SCHOOLS COUNCIL **WORKING PAPER 51**

Social education: an experiment in four secondary schools

the report of the Schools Council Social Education Project
based at the Institute of Education,
University of Nottingham

J. Rennie, E. A. Lunzer and W. T. Williams

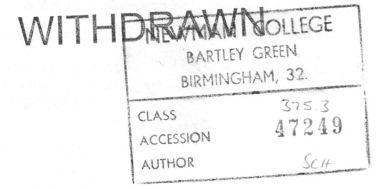
Evans / Methuen Educational

*First published 1974 for the Schools Council
by Evans Brothers Limited
Montague House, Russell Square, London WC1B 5BX
and Methuen Educational Limited
11 New Fetter Lane, London EC4P 4EE*

*Distributed in the US by Citation Press
Scholastic Magazines Inc., 50 West 44th Street
New York, NY 10036
and in Canada by Scholastic–TAB Publications Ltd
123 Newkirk Road
Richmond Hill, Ontario*

ISBN 0 423 49870 3

*Printed in Great Britain by
Richard Clay (The Chaucer Press) Ltd
Bungay, Suffolk*

Contents

Foreword   *page* 5

I   **Social education and the project**   7
Origins of the project   8
Aims of the project   10
Outline history of the project   11
Conclusion   15

II   **A programme of social education**   17
1. Introducing social education in the classroom   18
2. Teaching observation and communication: the use of socio-drama   19
3. Profiles   24
4. Recurrent themes   31
5. Identification leading to participation   33

III   **The work of the project: 1969–71**   36

IV   **Evaluation**   50
Introduction   50
Interviews with teachers   52
Pupil attitude to social education   64
Attitude to school   70
Impact on the community   78
Additional procedures   86
Summary and conclusion   89

V   **Social education in action**   91
1. Pupil responsibility   91
2. The role of the teacher   95
3. Surveys: preparation, execution and follow-up   97
4. Effect on the individual   101

VI   **Implementing social education**   105
1. Objections and replies   105
2. Introducing social education into the curriculum   112
3. Introducing social education: maximum or minimum
level   115
4. Co-operative teaching   116
5. Summary   117

VII   **Conclusions and recommendations**   119

Appendices   **A**   Project discussion papers   .   123
B   Syllabuses and reports from participating teachers   138
C   Evaluation: additional data   156

Foreword

Social education is undoubtedly a topic of growing interest to teachers. The Schools Council receives a steady and sometimes urgent stream of inquiries, not only about this particular project, but also about that ill-defined but evolving part of the curriculum which deals with education for social responsibility, with the school's relationship to its community and to society at large.

Social education is seen by many as a major component of any worth-while curriculum for all pupils, alongside the teaching of knowledge and skills in more traditional areas. From this wider perspective, the Social Education Project at Nottingham University will be seen as a pilot inquiry on a limited scale. It lasted only three years, for two of these three years it was restricted to four schools, and even within these schools, there were restrictions on the number of pupils involved as well as on the time devoted to the work. The project was also handicapped by the illness of its director, Professor Harry Davies, which prevented him from offering the close guidance he would have wished, although he was able none the less to ensure its operation along worth-while lines.

Despite these limitations this report may well be the most useful contribution to appear so far in this important field. Although the work of the project was limited in the ways described, it nevertheless represents a concerted effort to implement social education consistently and over a period. The ideas of Richard Hauser and previous trials by John Rennie and others based on these ideas provided the necessary groundwork. But they did not guarantee success. Nor was success uniformly achieved in all schools. The present volume gives a detailed account of difficulties and of opportunities, of obstacles and successes. Perhaps the greatest success was the active involvement of pupils of low ability and the feeling they gained of doing and learning something worth while.

The field of this report is not an easy one to evaluate. Research workers will therefore certainly find considerable interest in the chapter on evaluation, when a resolute attempt is made to overcome some of the problems. But there is a sense in which the whole of the report is an evaluation of the conditions necessary to make social education a success. It is for this reason that it should command the careful attention of all teachers and educationists who have an interest in the social relevance of their work.

5

Members of the project team

Professor H. Davies (Director)	Institute (now School) of Education, University of Nottingham
Dr J. C. Daniels (Acting director)	Institute of Education, University of Nottingham
John Rennie (Leader)	
E. J. K. Cordell (until July 1970)	Formerly Deputy Head, Sheerness Secondary Boys' School
W. T. Williams (from August 1970)	Institute of Education, University of Nottingham
Professor E. A. Lunzer (Evaluator)	Institute of Education, University of Nottingham

I. Social education and the project

One of the qualities of a good education is that it should enable young people to adapt successfully to the requirements of living in the conditions which face them now and will face them when their formal education is over. In modern society these requirements are many and complex, just as society itself is complex. Moreover society is constantly changing, and today's students are being educated for a kind of life which neither we nor they can foresee.

If our students are to fulfil roles in society which will bring satisfaction to themselves and be beneficial to others, education must not only help them in the development of personality and academic ability, but also provide them with the skills which are necessary to cope with a sophisticated and expanding technology. This is true even of those who will not be directly involved in development and design or in large-scale organization and planning. Equally, a good education should enable the student to cope with the increasingly bewildering pressures of life in a modern society. In a tribal community every member knows how the group is organized and how it achieves its ends, and every member plays a part. Much the same was true of the Greek city state – at least for its freemen. But, in modern urban society, government is remote and often seems incomprehensible. Even the interests and occupations of our neighbours can be a mystery. The individual is all too liable to feel isolated, trapped, manipulated by agencies which he cannot understand, even though they are benevolent. The problems that arise are mostly common problems but, owing to the insulation which is so characteristic of our society, the individual often cannot come to terms with them, let along take action to overcome them.

Social education is therefore an integral part of a full education, and without it there can be no adequate preparation for life. Of course, many features of schooling already help to meet this need. For instance, there is the ethos of the school which may be developed by the headteacher and staff through a free system of discipline and pupil participation in decision-making, by a genuine delegation of responsibility, by the maintenance of traditions of co-operative effort and tolerance, and in many other ways. There are also more specialized courses and services such as individual pupil guidance and counselling, careers guidance and work experience, leavers' courses, courses in environmental or social studies, religious and moral education, and so on. Finally, there are many projects whose aim is to make the curriculum more relevant to the pupils' interests and to the rich yet fluid structure of knowledge in the present century. The Schools Council's Humanities Curriculum Project is an outstanding example. But much of this is indirect teaching. The Schools Council's Social Education Project was conceived in the belief that preparation for life in the modern urban community warranted a more direct approach. Instead of a reliance on incidental learning, what was wanted was an explicit attempt to teach people an awareness of their surroundings, sensitivity to their own and to one another's problems, and an appreciation of how individuals can collaborate both to inform themselves and to better their own lot.

The concept of social education in this more specific sense was developed by Richard Hauser of the Centre for Group Studies in a series of lectures, discussions and papers. In the years since 1959 Hauser has been able to persuade many teachers of the relevance of such an education, and there have been numerous individual attempts to incorporate his ideas into the framework of the conventional curriculum. But such attempts are necessarily limited in their effect because they did not involve more than a few of a school's staff or a proportion of its pupils. Also, without expert backing and support the individual teacher can hardly be blamed if his enthusiasm tends to wear thin after a time: he may well take up some other idea or even lapse into less imaginative modes of teaching, because these are a great deal easier to use and may be more acceptable to colleagues.

If social education is to fulfil the aim of providing an adequate curriculum for social living, it must be a continuous process spread over the whole of a pupil's schooling. Nor is it sufficient for the principles of co-operation, initiative, self-direction and collective responsibility to be learned and practised in certain periods while the pupil remains subject to a traditional, even authoritarian, routine during the major part of a school week.

Origins of the project

While the idea of a school committed to social education was seen to have much to commend it, there was clearly a need for preliminary experiments in implementing such a concept. Would the idea of a curriculum geared to community problems be acceptable to schools? Would the pupils prove equal to assuming increased responsibility both for the form of their work and for its content? Would the problems of community living offer an adequate store of material for valid educational study? How far was it possible to introduce ideas and problems

8

in such a way as to capture the interest and imagination of younger pupils? Would the introduction of social education be likely to help in alleviating the problems of the community as a whole, to mitigate the alienation of some of its members, or even to bridge gaps between youth and the older generation, between home and school, between the school and the surrounding community?

Having listened to the arguments of Hauser and others, the Schools Council decided in 1968 to launch a trial project over a period of three years. A programme of social education would be implemented in a limited number of schools, with guidance and materials from a team of full-time workers, these being teachers who had considerable practical experience in the implementation of Hauser's ideas. The project was to be directed by the Institute of Education (now the School of Education) at Nottingham University, and the overall direction of the work would be in the hands of a small steering committee, under the chairmanship of Professor H. Davies, who was appointed project director.

Apart from the limited efforts of individuals already referred to, social education in Hauser's sense was new and untried. From its inception, therefore, the project was conceived as a very necessary piece of action research, rather than as a neatly packaged curriculum to be implemented in schools. It was realized from the outset that methods of working would be subject to change in the light of experience. It would be the major function of the steering committee to maintain a constant review of progress and to consider the desirability of changes. Among its members were headteachers in the project schools, representatives of local education authorities, the University and the Schools Council, and outside experts. Richard Hauser was a member of the steering committee and acted as adviser to the project, particularly in its earlier stages.

It should not be thought, however, that because a need for changes was foreseen at the start, the project began as no more than a leap in the dark. Without clear perception of aims, and without some guide-lines as to likely methods, no project would have been possible. Both were available from previous work by Richard Hauser and his associates. Almost equally important, previous experience had indicated some of the difficulties that the project would face and steps were taken early to overcome them. The following sections deal more specifically with the aims of the project, its history and its outcome. These sections will, however, be brief, since the history of the project is treated more fully in the remainder of the report.

Aims of the project

Social education is seen by Hauser as 'an enabling process, through which children will receive a sense of identification with their community, become sensitive to its shortcomings, and develop methods of participation in those activities needed for the solution of social problems'.

Its intention is to counteract the sense of social ineffectiveness experienced within our society, and the isolation which characterizes the lives of so many of its members. Social improvement is seen not as the manipulation of regulations or the handing out of aid to those in need. Active social participation in communal affairs is held to be a necessary (perhaps even a sufficient) condition for a satisfactory social existence. It follows that social education can only come about through the exercise of responsibility. Children will learn a sense of community involvement only by being involved in the conditions of their own social existence, that is in the elaboration of their own curriculum and in the planning of their own school work.

Social education should not be confused with the concept of the free school. A free school is one in which each individual pupil is allowed to do what he pleases with the minimum of constraints, while the staff provide curricular facilities and facilities for idleness. Its hope is that pupils will soon tire of frivolous activities, and will turn to serious studies of their own free choice and volition. Individual motivation will then bring an individual sense of achievement and spur the pupil to more effective learning than would the discipline of the formal school. The ideal which animates the free school movement is that of a liberal democracy in which the individual is left maximally free from the constraints of government, government itself being a necessary evil to be mitigated by giving to all an equal say in periodic elections. By contrast, a school committed to social education is one in which staff and pupils are engaged in common pursuits which have been collectively agreed. Far from being left free to 'do his own thing', the individual is charmed and pressured into active participation in group activities. On the other hand, these activities are not imposed by the staff. They are evolved by the pupils themselves with some staff guidance, and while this may be considerable to begin with, the very essence of the process requires that such guidance be progressively diminished. The ideal which animates social education harks back to an older concept of democracy: the democracy (real or legendary) of the Greek city state in which the chief pursuit of citizens was deemed to be their participation in running their collective affairs. Modern counterparts might be sought in Cuba, in China or in the Israeli kibbutzim.

Such examples are remote from Britain in time or place, and in the political and economic framework in which they exist, and they are disparate from one another. Moreover each may be open to criticism on different grounds and from different points of view. It follows that the wider aim of social education is one whose realization cannot be guaranteed. We simply do not know how far it is possible to bring about a generalized active involvement in the community within the context of modern urban and metropolitan living. Nor can we say what changes this might entail in the political and economic framework of society, if it were capable of complete achievement. One is certainly more sceptical than was once the case about the promise of achieving massive social change by mere educational reform. Project Headstart* has been an inspiring, but in some ways a discouraging example.

But the problems of alienation and isolation are too acute to be ignored. Closely bound up with them is the educational problem of the irrelevance of schooling as seen by at least a third of its recipients. In the context of these problems, the Social Education Project was a very tentative step in a potentially rewarding direction. Its aim was to explore how far it was possible to achieve a less one-sided education, a more active pupil participation and a greater awareness and involvement in relation to community affairs, by encouraging a programme of social education in a limited number of schools. The programme was initially designed to include work within the community as well as work within the schools. So far as the pupils were concerned, some estimate of the success of such a project might be gained from the record of its implementation, from the satisfaction of the pupils who participated in it and from the comments made by the teachers themselves. But, if really successful, the project should reach beyond the school and affect the outside community, its cohesiveness and its sense of purpose.

Outline history of the project

The work of the project fell into two phases.

The first was an experimental trial phase in 1968–9. During this preliminary period an attempt was made to initiate social education programmes in ten schools in the Nottingham area. In addition, almost equal emphasis was placed

* A programme for the economically disadvantaged pre-school child, initiated by the United States Office of Economic Opportunity and operating in 1967 and the years immediately following. See *Disadvantaged Child*, ed. Jerome Hellmuth, Vol. 3: Compensatory Education: a National Debate (Brunner/Mazel, New York, 1970).

on the dissemination of ideas to teachers in training with the co-operation of the Nottingham Regional College of Technology (now Trent Polytechnic), and serving teachers seconded to Diploma Courses at the Institute of Education. Only one full-time worker, John Rennie, was appointed. In addition, one part-time associate was engaged to help in the task of introducing new concepts and modes of work in the schools concerned, while another would help to establish contacts with agencies in the community. Both of these were employed for one day a week only. So far as the work in schools was concerned, it was hoped that a programme of lectures and discussions given at the teachers' centre in Nottingham, coupled with demonstration lessons by John Rennie and his colleagues, might be sufficient to enable participant schools to go forward on their own and develop whatever methods of work were most suitable to their particular needs and circumstances.

Achievement in this period was limited. Some lesson programmes were shown to be successful and, in the main, the goodwill of the schools was retained. But the experience was mainly useful in highlighting difficulties. Neither discussions (not always well attended), nor demonstrations were enough. There was a marked tendency for the effort in schools to be sporadic. In addition, the outline programmes devised by the project staff were often treated as no more than a set of alternative topics to interest leavers' classes and backward streams, without regard to the requirements of pupil involvement and self-direction. Work within the community had been largely limited to liaison, and little of substance had been negotiated.

It was therefore decided to concentrate the activities of the project in four schools. Also, an additional full-time worker was appointed to assist John Rennie.* This reduction in the number of schools and the doubling of the full-time staff permitted fundamental changes in the method of work.

Three of the original ten schools were retained. Because all the schools had shown a willingness to co-operate, the choice of these three was difficult. The selection was based in part on the desirability of retaining some variety in the type of school involved, and partly upon the expressed interest of the teachers concerned. The fourth school was one which had not been involved in the first year of the project. It was selected for two reasons. First, the school is un-streamed and this enabled the work to be attempted in a different kind of structure from all the other schools, thus adding an interesting variable. Second, the headmaster and several teachers in this school had expressed an interest in the

* Keith Cordell held the second post during 1969–70. In July 1970 he left to take up an appointment in Sheppey and was succeeded by Wyn Williams, who held the post until the completion of the project.

project's work and had maintained contact with the project for several months during the first year.

The schools were of different types, serving vastly differing communities. One was a single-sex bilateral school serving an overspill council estate; another was a mixed secondary modern serving a village which had recently undergone rapid growth through an influx of miners; another, a mixed bilateral school, served a city-centre redevelopment area; the fourth, a mixed secondary modern, served an urban mining area.

In the unstreamed school, the project classes consisted of the whole group in each of two years. In the streamed schools, the classes were the lowest streams in their particular year group. At first it was expected that the work in each school would be identical, but in the event quite fundamental differences emerged. The kind of work attempted in any school is determined to some extent by the structures operating in that school – that is, streaming or non-streaming, subject-based timetable or integrated studies, single-period lessons or block timetabling, etc. Other major factors which influence the work are the talents, interests and attitudes of the teaching staff, and not least the area in which the school is situated. So it was with the work of the project in these four schools.

In three of the schools the work was felt to be a qualified success, though in quite different ways. In one school, although the ultimate aim of children's involvement in their community was not achieved, the work done within the school captured the imagination of the children and they revealed a considerable depth of understanding. One of the evaluation measures used was designed to test attitudes to social education. This school scored highly on this test in comparison with the other three project schools. In a further test designed to measure attitudes to school, the children from this school showed the most favourable attitude of twelve schools which were given the test (four project schools and eight control schools). In particular, averages for self-concept as successful pupils and appreciation of teacher were the highest in all twelve schools.

In the second of the three schools where the work was considered to be a qualified success, the children did become involved in their community. Unlike the first school, the one which joined the project at the end of its first year, this school worked with the project for three years, which perhaps accounts for this difference. Despite the fact that the ethos of this school was less favourable (in terms which are discussed later) to the implementation of social education, its attitudes to social education revealed a depth of involvement greater than that obtained in any other school. This is perhaps best illustrated with reference to

13

the part of the evaluation designed to test impact on the community. For this test, a series of interviews with parents and residents of each of the four communities was carried out. Social education was not mentioned in all cases, although where it was it invariably met with approval. The interviews carried out in the area of this school produced a higher number of responses revealing knowledge of the project, and stronger expressions of approval of the work. They included one or two quite remarkable unsolicited testimonials concerning the importance of social education and its effect on children.

In the third of the three schools, the children achieved a much smaller degree of involvement in the community, although there can be no doubting their interest in such involvement. However, they did produce a considerable amount of imaginative work within the school. In the test on attitude to school, their average score was the second highest among the twelve schools tested.

The fourth school did not become involved in its community at any stage. For a variety of reasons, the work of the project team in this school never coalesced into a coherent whole. Because of changes in the organizational structure of the school, very few children in the class who did social education in the fourth year of their school life had taken part in the work done during the two previous years. This meant that the process described in Chapter II was never experienced by the vast majority of the children. The resultant fragmentary nature of the work is perhaps reflected in their response to the test asking for their definitions of social education and attitudes towards it. This test shows that they saw social education as a series of unconnected topics, and not as a whole. Although the majority of children were favourable towards social education, a much higher proportion than in other schools revealed an unfavourable or neutral attitude towards it.

While it is important to consider the objective evidence provided by these tests, the more subjective evaluation of the teachers involved needs to be borne in mind. From the evidence of diaries kept by the teachers, which are quoted later in this report, and from very frequent contacts by the project team with these teachers, it is clear that not only did teachers feel that the content and approaches suggested by the project were important and relevant to the needs of their children, but that the children had been interested and had benefited from such work. As proof of this belief, a group of these teachers have started and developed a working party which continues to meet on Saturday mornings at regular intervals. The group is also collaborating in the in-service training of teachers.

The Social Education Project is one of a series mounted by the Schools Council in its concern to develop programmes suitable for implementation

14

following the raising of the school-leaving age. During the development of the project, however, it became increasingly obvious both to the project team and to teachers in the school that, if this work is to be successful in the final year of school life, it needs to be based on work completed at a much earlier age. It must be seen as a process which begins at the start of a child's secondary education, and very probably well before, and continues at least until he leaves school.

In addition to the work carried on in schools, a further element of the project's work was concerned with the in-service training of teachers involved in studies for the Advanced Diploma in Education of the University of Nottingham. More than thirty teachers opted for a social education course in each of the three years during which the project lasted. Each of these groups was maintained throughout the twelve-month duration of the course, and each expressed a firm belief in the necessity for such work. In addition, the project team undertook many in-service commitments in teachers' centres and universities in various parts of the country, as well as work with students undergoing initial teacher training. Most of these were, of necessity, limited to a single session and the project team was able to meet only a small proportion of the requests made.

Conclusion

The widespread interest aroused by the project gives some indication of the reality of the need which social education seeks to fulfil. Taken as a whole, the experience of the project team leads us to believe that the conception is valid. Moreover social education has both a specific and a general aspect. Specifically, it may involve a concentrated effort through the years of secondary schooling to acquaint pupils with the circumstances of their social environment and to equip them with such skills as are necessary for them to play a full part in shaping it to their collective advantage. More generally, it entails a joint responsibility on the part of teachers, pupils and parents to ensure that what is done at school should be relevant to the pupil even after he has left. The responsibility is a joint one, since social education is incompatible with the view that the curriculum should be determined by the teacher alone. From this more general standpoint, the ideals of social education would necessarily affect all that is done in a school committed to its realization.

These conclusions are set out in more detail in Chapter VII. The full report of the project which leads to these conclusions occupies the intervening chapters. Chapter II consists of a detailed programme for the implementation of the specifically curricular aspect of social education. It was the programme which the team endeavoured to realize in the four project schools. Chapter III is an account of how the programme was implemented in each of the schools concerned. Chapter IV contains a statement of the measures taken to evaluate the process of the work, together with quantitative and qualitative results. In none of the schools was the programme realized in full, and Chapters V and VI describe some of the difficulties that the team had to face, as well as presenting instances of particular opportunities that came as the work proceeded. The material contained in these chapters is taken directly from records kept by teachers, pupils and members of the project team.

It is hoped that the inclusion of these examples will prove useful to those who wish to attempt similar programmes elsewhere.

II. A programme of social education

The object of this chapter is to give an account of some methods of realizing the aims of the project, in sufficient detail to enable the reader to begin to formulate a programme of his own, should he wish to do so. A secondary object is to provide him with a clear statement of the set of ideas which animated the project workers in their day-to-day work within the schools involved, so as to give some meaning to the account of what in fact was achieved. However, ideas are subject to change, particularly when they are relatively untried and one begins to put them into practice. It would be possible, but difficult now, to try to recapture the state of our ideas at the beginning of the project. However, a partial statement of aims, made available to all concerned at the inception of the project, is reproduced in Appendix A2. We prefer here to update the programme in the light of the knowledge gained in the course of its implementation. It is hoped that such a statement will prove more useful because it is more realistic. Indeed, from time to time the experience of actual lessons given in the course of the project will be used to give flesh and blood to the programme in this chapter.

Of the five sections that follow, the first takes up again the problem announced briefly in Chapter I, which is that of promoting self-reliance and self-direction in pupils whose self-image may well have been impaired and distorted by the experience of failure in school – as was undoubtedly true of the majority of the boys and girls who formed the target of the experimental project. A number of techniques are included which have been found useful in dealing with this situation. The next section is concerned with the first stage in the process of social education: training in observation and communication. It includes a full description of one of the principal techniques which is used extensively at this stage, and from time to time throughout the programme, the technique of socio-drama. The third section deals with the three consecutive areas of study which can be used to enlarge the field of awareness and involvement: the class, the school and the area. The fourth section is devoted to two of the principal themes treated in the course of the social education programme: man–woman relationships, and crises of personal responsibility. The fifth section is concerned with the final stage of the programme: participation in the community and its affairs.

17

1. Introducing social education in the classroom

Social education takes place in all schools, whatever their ethos. The way the school is organized, streamed or not streamed, the role of examinations in the school, the way teachers speak to children, the way children treat each other, the prefect system, the house system, all these tell children something about their place in the school and what the school stands for.

Clearly not every school provides the ideal setting for introducing a specific programme in social education designed to promote responsibility and involvement. For in some schools at any rate, the 'hidden curriculum' of social education will have been more conducive to that mixture of conformity and apathy which is the exact antithesis of what is proposed. However, let us suppose an ideal setting. Imagine what would be the most appropriate school structure and value system for social education to operate successfully. The school would be non-authoritarian in that decisions would be reached by a process which involved all teaching, domestic and clerical staff and also the pupils, since all would be affected by those decisions. Mixed ability groups would replace streaming so that no child is identified as a failure. Staff would operate in teams, with two objectives: first, to enable all staff to participate in planning and implementing curricula; second, to enable a holistic approach to education to develop through the integration of subjects. Even given such a school, the teacher is still faced with creating a classroom environment conducive to the development of children's skills in coping with the demands made upon them by this type of school structure.

The social structure of most classrooms may be described as that of a crowd. A crowd is a minimum undifferentiated form of group, as opposed to a group proper, which presupposes both some degree of internal differentiation and a network of relations with other groups. A class is usually regarded as a single group. It is treated as a whole, with no conscious regard paid to the sub-groups within the class, or to their *de facto* leaders. This virtually ensures that the teacher must become the imposed, paternalistic (at best) leader of the class. Gifted teachers may be able to evoke group patterns of loyalty and interest; they rarely attempt deliberately to produce a genuine group culture. Whether or not the stern disciplinarian attitude is appropriate is another question. Our main argument is that social education cannot be taught effectively by the paternalistic teacher because the behaviours that are characteristic of a crowd are alien to the growth of democratic values.

To introduce social education as an exercise in applied democracy inevitably entails new learning for teachers as well as pupils, and there are no easy short cuts. Given the ideal setting, the exercise is made much smoother. But less ideal settings need not preclude attempts to begin the social education process – the attempt to introduce social education may well cause the setting itself to move closer to the desired image.

We turn now to a second problem, and one that was particularly acute in the project schools. In general, the pupils engaged in social education were taken from the lowest ability groups. Their self-confidence had already been sapped and their willingness to display initiative in the school setting had been drained by their previous failure. They had to be made to feel that past 'failures' in academic work were not signs of uselessness or stupidity on their part. In order to do this, children were encouraged to think of intelligence as having four parts: abstract intelligence which enables us to understand abstract concepts; technical intelligence which allows us to remember processes; creative intelligence which enables us to create new ideas and things; and social intelligence which enables us to understand people and relationships.

Such a four-fold division of intelligence is not without psychological validity, although the concept would doubtless require considerable re-phrasing to be acceptable to psychologists. Psychologists might prefer to think of areas of information-processing and decision-making and the various demands that these make on the individual. They would certainly question the explicit reification of four distinct 'faculties'. But the object of the lesson was a practical one. It was to break down the sense of failure, and to encourage pupils to start afresh in fields where they had received little or no previous stimulation – that is, the creative and social fields.

2. Teaching observation and communication: the use of socio-drama

As early as possible in the secondary school, building on activities in the primary school, much basic work needs to be done to develop the complementary skills of observation and communication. If we do not 'observe', if we are not 'aware', then our capacity to participate in a situation is severely reduced. Communication skills are essential if what has been observed is to be fully understood. Observation and communication are the principal techniques that the child must acquire to enable him to advance in the process of social education. He must learn to pick out things that are significant and important in the social life about him. He must learn to interpret clues: how people reveal their attitudes by their behaviour, how they express their hopes and their fears. He must learn to ask questions in ways which at once show and promote understanding. He must learn to communicate his own feelings and reactions and to share them with others.

19

For all these purposes it has been found that a technique of dramatic improvisation applied to specific social themes is peculiarly well-suited. This technique, termed 'socio-drama', is social in two senses: not only is the content chosen for its social significance, but its aim, too, is to promote understanding rather than technical skills in dramatic performance. Known also as 'role-playing' or 'improvised drama', socio-drama has presented problems to teachers, in that even the more experienced teachers of subjects other than English have sometimes lacked the confidence to attempt to use it.

As with social education itself, effective socio-drama situations can only be achieved by developing skills systematically, and teachers have found great difficulties when they have tried short cuts, and have expected children to be able to participate without having learned these skills.

It may be necessary, depending upon how much children have been used to miming, to begin with very simple mimes, and the teacher needs to exercise his judgement to determine the appropriate level at which his class is capable of operating. Some examples of such mimes are:

> come here (I am angry with you)
> come here (I have something to show you)
> fear (in a dark room)
> terror (attacked by a vicious dog)
> wonderful news
> surprise.

If the class is divided into small groups, with each group being given a number of such situations, it means that everybody is quickly given an opportunity to participate, without the embarrassment of 'performing' in front of a large group.

The next stage would involve miming everyday situations with which children are familiar, for example:

> pouring tea
> making a bed
> cleaning shoes
> receiving and greeting a visitor
> brushing teeth, etc.

An element of fun can be brought in by making a game of this observation work, for example:

> Ask six children to go out of the room, knock at the door one by one, come in, close the door and sit down. The class then discuss the different actions of the six.

20

Ask a number of pupils to mime how the head, a new boy, a prefect, would come in at the door.

Again in small groups, with the observers criticizing and correcting, the situations to be mimed are now developed further, and a social element appears:

helping a toddler to cross the road
mother calls in disobedient boy
helping mother at washing machine/drying dishes
very heavy basket carried by an old lady
helping a blind man to cross the road
helping a pedestrian who has fainted
serving a meal to a sick or aged person.

When pupils have mastered mime sufficiently well, group situations may be presented where pupils are encouraged to show feeling and consideration for others:

crowd on bus – an old lady gets on the bus
crowd crossing street – including a small child
fight in street – a man injured
people in flat – someone mentions lonely old lady in another flat
crowd at bus stop – suddenly it starts raining – small children and old person in queue.

Teachers of English will be very familiar with these methods of building skills, although their aim is less likely to have such a social element, for they would be concerned with the development of these skills for their own sake.

Once mime has developed into simple forms of drama, situation 'tests' can be tackled. Situations are described on slips of paper and distributed to the groups. At first, the situation tests should be fairly straightforward. There is no moral conflict, but the actor must consider what is the appropriate action. The solution is not confined to one person and several are asked 'What would you do?':

if the heater overturned and the carpet was set alight when you were left alone with your baby brother
if there was a gas leak
if the tap failed to close and you could not locate the mains tap
if the iron started smouldering or sparking
if you were alone in your father's car and it started moving
if baby brother swallowed a big sweet
if you heard a noise at your window at night

21

if you woke up and found yourself alone in the house
if you smelt something burning
if you had to return home from the seaside but found you had lost your money.

To each of the above there will be a variety of answers and pupils will discuss each slip vigorously and analyse each one before deciding on the most sensible course of action.

In the next set of situations, much more complex activities and motives and moral standards are brought to the surface:

returning a pair of shoes, which are found to be unsuitable, to a shop
manager interviewing young man for a job
boy persuading father to buy a new cycle
explaining and apologizing for broken window to owner of a house
boy falsely accused explains situation to a teacher
explaining to parents why a particular style of clothing should be bought
explaining to policeman why cycle is defective
tickets lost – explain situation to manager of theatre
convincing youth club members that social project should be undertaken (plight of old people, etc.)
interview with council official – need for play street
a young man asking girl to go to a dance with him
complaint to hairdresser.

The situation can be enlarged to include any number of pupils. 'Who thinks this?' 'Who thinks that?' 'What would you do now?' 'Why wouldn't you do this?' This type of questioning makes people think, and pupils are less prone to accept answers blindly and unquestioningly.

Eventually, children can attempt quite complex social situations with, perhaps, four or five sets of conflicting interests involved. Thus, a family difficulty in which a brother and younger sister have conflicting interests, into which are brought mother, father and even grandparents, can provide an advanced socio-drama situation. Through the spontaneous working out in improvised dramatization of familiar social episodes, youngsters will often purge themselves of a surprising amount of unhappiness and self-doubt. It enables them to live through, in advance and in a make-believe setting, many of the difficulties of communication which they will face in the future. By the time a pupil reaches his fourth year, the content of these improvised dramatizations will have become more complex, for example:

an immigrant family moves into the area – the son comes to your youth club and falls into an argument with one of your friends;

22

father insists that you come in at ten o'clock, but allows your older brother to stay out later;

a neighbour asks you to look after her children while she visits her husband in hospital – you have promised to go out with your friends;

on starting work, you are picked on by a boy who started last year – the foreman sees him, but seems to ignore it.

For many children, even the simplest of the earlier situations will prove challenging, so they need to be simple enough to allow the child the success from which he will gain the confidence to try out more adventurous tasks later. Once the initial breakthrough has been made and a class is prepared to tackle socio-drama, much of the work can be related to the profiles and surveys which the children will by then be undertaking. For instance, a family conflict situation such as the second example above would clearly be done when the class were building their family profile.

The approach sets out to activate the mind by developing and training the child's latent powers of observation and, most important, by developing functional intelligence and thus providing the child with a desire to learn, read and record; he begins to analyse his own conduct and that of others and by degrees to learn to assert himself and see himself as part of the social pattern and gain success and dignity by participating in it.

Needless to say, as with anything worth while, there are dangers to be borne in mind. First, it is no use expecting children to launch straight into socio-drama without adequate preparation in observation and communication, and in mime. Second, children should not be pushed into participating in activities for which they are unready or unwilling. In any class there will be children at several stages of development in their ability to participate. Third, the teacher needs to know his class sufficiently well to be able to avoid putting children into situations which they may find difficult or embarrassing. If a child has no father, he may well be upset by being asked to take part in a situation where there is conflict between father and son. This is another reason why small group work is so valuable. It enables the teacher to set the situation and to leave the children to choose their own roles and their own solutions.

Fourth, it is important to remember that these skills will take some time to develop and that the final stages will not be reached until the third or fourth year of secondary school. Because the children enjoy this work so much, there is a danger that teachers will concentrate too much on this aspect, to the detriment of other aspects of the work.

Fifth, it is important to stress the vital necessity for children to be given the opportunity to discuss and to criticize these socio-dramas, not from an 'acting' point of view, but from the point of view of the social implications of what they have seen or taken part in. Too often, teachers are tempted to be satisfied with the fact that children have enjoyed the socio-drama, and to leave them to draw their own conclusions, thus missing the opportunity for vigorous, stimulating and fruitful discussion.

It is true to say that where teachers have felt some trepidation in attempting socio-drama, it has largely been because of their unawareness of the preliminary stages. When these stages have been gone through, teachers have found very few problems in their work.

3. Profiles

Profiles are attempts to enable children to look in depth at the structure of groups which have immediate impact upon them. Thus the major groups which are studied are the school class, the family, the school, the peer group and ultimately the local community. Because we aim to allow children to develop ideas of their own, each of these profiles may well inspire other aspects of study. During the project, for example, profiles have led various classes to studies of heredity, the generation gap, pollution and conservation, minority groups and scapegoatism, various aspects of local history, pressure groups and the problems of redevelopment areas.

The profiles have always been built by small groups within a class or a year group following their own particular interest and contributing towards the whole, thus giving greater width to each one. Each of the profiles takes weeks to build and includes as many different points of view as possible. The results are always recorded, using different media, and presented in the school and elsewhere. Film, videotape, photography, creative writing, graphs, drawings, diagrams and tape-recordings have all been used in presenting the work. This presentation is considered to be essential, as it is felt that it adds prestige and status to the child's work, and places him in a success situation with which he may be all too unfamiliar.

THE CLASS PROFILE

The class profile has four main aims:

a   to develop basic skills of observation and communication: looking, listening, describing, conversing, writing, illustrating;

24

b   to enable children to understand the structure and significance of the various sub-groups within the class;

c   to enable children to have a clear understanding of the duties and responsibilities of themselves and their fellows;

d   to enable children to learn the skills and techniques required for more advanced profiles of the school, community, etc., to be introduced later in the programme.

Many different methods have been used to explore various items of the profile, and no attempt will be made here to describe them all or even to say which has been most effective. This is because it is felt that teachers will be more successful if they apply their own methods, and one conclusion that we have been able to draw from observing different approaches to the profiles is that there are many effective methods. So many external factors affect the teaching – e.g. the relationship of staff and pupils, the age and attitudes of pupils, the facilities in the school and perhaps above all the needs of the children – that it would be invidious to select any one method as the ideal.

The usual starting-point is for the teacher to ask for suggestions from the class as to which aspect of their group they would be interested in studying. This normally produces a mass of ideas which are then sifted and selected by the class in their small groups. The teacher's task is to try to avoid unnecessary duplication, to encourage, to provide resources, to give advice and to stimulate. It is not to direct either the course of study or the methods of collation and presentation. That is to say, he is an enabler.

One class in a project school chose the following areas of study:

photographs of the class now, and as children
heights and weights
autographs and fingerprints
hobbies and interests
family trees
map to show where everyone in the class lives
birthplaces of class members and their parents
hair samples and colour of eyes
meanings of names of class members
pocket money
favourite television programmes
religions
map to show where class members spent their holidays over the last three years

survey of likes and dislikes under various headings (food, clothes, music, personalities, etc.).

Other classes have covered, between them, many more aspects than this. We found that in one year group, where a number of classes made a class profile at the same time, there was a surprising variation between the classes, not only in the areas of interest studied, but also in the methods of study and particularly in the methods adopted to present their results.

The whole profile is not merely a matter of data collected: it provides numerous educational opportunities. Socio-drama (e.g. conflict situations within a class or with the teacher, or mock interviews), discussion of class attitudes, creative writing based on classroom situations, the election of a class committee may all be undertaken concurrently.

Obviously, the more techniques that are used for exhibition purposes, the more demanding and challenging the exhibition becomes to exhibitors and spectators alike. Films, tape-recordings, models and photographs can be stimulating additions to the more conventional diagrams, graphs, creative writings, drawings and paintings.

The final stage in working on the class profile is for the whole class to look at the complete exhibition and for each small group to discuss and explain its own findings. This ensures that children who have been absorbed in several activities in some depth will not remain ignorant of what other groups have achieved. Frequently it results in children suggesting further lines of inquiry which the class usefully follow as a result of this work.

THE SCHOOL PROFILE

The school profile involves the children in considering the school from every conceivable point of view. On the factual side this includes its physical structure, numbers of staff and pupils, distribution of staff, sizes of various age-groups, number of clubs and societies and size of their membership, number who take school meals, use school buses, etc. More interestingly, perhaps, the children look at the roles of people in the school from three points of view. What are their duties, imposed upon them from above? What are their responsibilities, determined by themselves, and coming over and above the 'call of duty'? What are the relationships between the people in the school, and how do these affect individuals and groups?

One of the problems for the teacher is deciding when it is appropriate to do a school profile. A successful class profile is more likely to lead to follow-up work related to, say, a family profile than to a school profile. For example, one class wanted to take further the reasons for the differences in hair and eye colourings, i.e. they wanted to learn about heredity.

The introduction to the school profile needs to be deliberately thought out by the teacher. It is possible to begin by mounting an exhibition on 'what school is for' based on material like Edward Blishen's *The School That I'd Like* (Penguin Educational Special, Penguin Books, 1969) or Royston Lambert's *The Hothouse Society* (Weidenfeld & Nicolson, 1968). This is quite likely to provoke questions about school which can provide the stimulus for a profile.

Another approach is to wait for the incident which occurs in the classroom. One group were incensed by what they regarded as the unfair punishment of a boy. Here, the indignation felt could be guided into an examination of the disciplinary system, its workings and relationship to the whole school structure. On another occasion, 4D's statement that D stood for 'Dustbin' was the kind of remark that it is important to develop constructively, rather than allowing them to go on feeling that their place is at the bottom of the pile in an environment over which they have no control.

In undertaking a profile there are a number of stages to be gone through. The first job is a discussion to identify what is to be studied. In particular, the group will determine whether there is a hypothesis to be tested or a situation to be investigated (say the workings of the disciplinary system). Once the area of investigation is decided upon the class can divide into groups opting for specific tasks. Thus in one school a group prepared a questionnaire to examine what attitudes children had to the school; another group looked at the views of the staff and people like the governors and the caretaker by means of interviews; another group looked at facilities; another at the relationship between the feeder junior schools and the secondary school; while yet another group interviewed members of the public, including shopkeepers, bus conductors, etc., to see how they felt about the school.

The preparation stage for carrying out the questionnaire and interviewing involves mock interviews, dummy runs of questionnaires, and socio-drama to illustrate difficult situations which might arise when talking to adults. One group was faced with an interview in which the parks inspector launched into a tirade against teenage vandalism. To anticipate and prepare for this kind of situation is vital.

The collecting of information is followed by its presentation in as many striking and intelligible forms as the group can conceive. The techniques employed in doing the class profile are obviously useful.

Once presentation by the groups has been completed, the class will proceed to

27

an analysis of the findings to identify areas of concern. This may well result in proposals for action, or a hypothesis may be developed which can be tested in a survey. Thus, in the school profile discussed above the conclusion was drawn that one solution to the inadequate ideas about the secondary school held by parents and children was to prepare a booklet for them setting out clearly what they should expect. Another idea was for secondary children to visit and work in feeder junior schools.

AREA PROFILE

A profile of an area may comprise any of the following:

a *Where we live*
   describing our neighbourhood: residential areas, factories, shops, etc.
   the street: neighbours, ages, children
   our customs: the way we live, weekends and holidays
   neighbours in difficulty: the elderly, cripples, chronic sick
   local characters
   relations who live near: grandpa, grandma, uncles, aunts (and friends).

b *How we play – what we do after four o'clock*
   clubs we belong to: what we do there, games, how many attend, age-range, how often do we go, do we enjoy it, how would we improve it?
   places to play unsupervised: parks, waste ground, football pitches, play streets
   where do we meet our friends: the gang, what do we do?
   where are we not allowed to play and why (are we or others likely to get into trouble in danger areas, old buildings, railway lines, private property)?
   where do we go on Saturday afternoons: what for, alone or with friends, are we likely to get into trouble, why?

c *Local problems*
   dangerous roads, derelict areas
   transport: bus shelters, frequency of buses, bus stops
   old people: housing problems, bad landlords.

d *Authority*
   where is the police station in our area?
   relationships with the police: policeman's usual beat, does he move us on, why?

28

park-keepers, uniformed attendants, local busybodies
relationships with people near where we play: old people, do they tell us
to play elsewhere, why?
any unpleasant people who frighten us or chase us.

e *The Church*
where are the churches in our area, which denominations?
which church do we go to: how many go, which denomination, do we go
alone or with friends?
what local charities are there, do we help, how?

f *Emergency services*
ambulance stations, hospital, fire station, doctor's surgery, police station
local people who help in emergencies
Civil Defence, Red Cross, St John Ambulance.

g *Who are the leaders in our area?*
the spokesmen for other peoples' problems: the councillor, the vicar, the
youth leader, the doctor, others.

h *Different age-groups*
where do the grown-ups, our parents, meet to gossip: the street corner,
local shop, the pub, the church hall, launderette, any other place?
where do the old people go to meet?
where do the young wives with babies go to meet?

i *Minority groups*
are there any newcomers in our neighbourhood: Indians, Pakistanis, West
Indians, Italians, Irish? how have they been made welcome, do people talk
about them, are they disliked, do we play with their children?
are there any gipsies: where do they live, have we met any, what do we
think of them, are they made welcome, if not, who moves them on?
are there any tramps or people sleeping rough, where, how do they live,
where do they get their money, are they made welcome by our neighbourhood, are they disliked, why?

From the above, we can see the width of the area profile. What is not shown
is the learning process which the children go through in building it. It should not
be regarded or conducted as a survey, a mere fact-finding exercise. In doing the

area profile, the children will be called upon to use many of the skills of argument, observation, interviewing, descriptive writing and speech which we hope will have been developed earlier. Some of the small groups in the class may well feel that they wish to show what happens in certain circumstances by giving a socio-drama for the rest of the class to comment on. Fundamental questions concerning the values of the local community in general may be raised.

As the work progresses, so one may begin to see the first glimpses of particular concerns developing in the children. From their work on this profile spring the more specific interests which lead to the surveys. We have quite often found that children wanted to take some action as a direct result of their area profile. All that was needed after the profile was a gathering of evidence or ideas to help guide their action, rather than the fuller survey which we describe later.

From the teacher's point of view, this stage is often the most difficult part of the whole social education process. Will he be able to recognize these early signs of a developing concern, and give the children the opportunities to come to decisions about what they do? Should he manage to do this, will he then be confident enough to give the children their heads in taking action? We have found that even those teachers who have a close and stable relationship with their class have found the task of avoiding direction of the children, while maintaining the role of experienced adviser, a difficult one. Support from headteacher and colleagues can be crucial here, and this underlines the value of a team approach. The clash between the naïve inventiveness of children and the sophisticated apprehension of even a committed adult must not be resolved by the latter's reverting to a paternalistic role. It is fair to say that the success of the whole process will now depend upon the familiarity with, and skill in employing, the democratic procedures which will necessarily have been practised for some con-siderable time, and in a variety of situations.

Opportunities for children to develop new lines of inquiry must be given at all stages. During the project, an area profile led on to an inquiry into pollution and conservation by one class. The family profile led to work on the generation gap by another class. Other developments took place at various stages in different schools, developments which were important in their own right, but which assumed added significance because they arose out of the children's ideas.

However, not all the elements of this process come from the children. The skilled teacher may decide when a particular line of inquiry will be followed, even if his decision will be influenced by the interests of the children at any particular stage. He thus creates the situation within which the pupils are given a considerable freedom to develop their own ideas. The amount of structuring of any particular line of inquiry which the teacher imposes will depend upon several factors, such as his relationship with the class, their level of maturity, the type of inquiry.

4. Recurrent themes

It will be apparent from the foregoing that the selection of successive areas for profile studies should in no way limit the day-to-day and week-to-week topics to be investigated under the heading of social education. The profiles provide an overall framework and a general sense of direction. Within this the teacher is encouraged to exploit whatever interests are suggested by the pupils themselves and to deal with them in whatever ways appear most fruitful. The same theme may be thrown up on several occasions, and this is particularly true of two topics which arose repeatedly in the course of the project. One was the general idea of man–woman relationships.

The method used by the project to introduce this topic to children was to identify for them five elements of the man–woman relationship which together make or break the relationship. These were identified as (a) common values – the extent to which a couple share the same beliefs, (b) partnership – the extent to which a couple share decision-making, (c) sex – sexual intercourse, (d) tenderness – all that part of a relationship ranging from a loving glance to what happens immediately before sexual intercourse, and (e) the nest – the extent to which a couple share a desire to build their home. These elements were not ranked, they were presented to the children in varying order.

The group would begin by a study of what is meant by each of these elements, using a variety of techniques: film, books, discussion in groups, discussion with the teacher. Discussion would then extend to the different ways in which relationships might vary and still provide a stable basis for love and mutual regard. To take an example: partnership, to be successful, does not necessarily mean that all decisions have to be taken together, with both partners sharing equally in the process. Provided that one partner is content in such a situation, the relationship would be equally successful if the other partner were dominant in this area of their relationship. The same is true of the other four elements. This approach proved extremely effective in stimulating discussion and breaks away from the increasingly common emphasis on sex instruction in schools, which often ignores so many important aspects of the man–woman relationship.

A second theme which was prominent throughout the work of the project was reaction to responsibility. When a person finds himself faced with new responsibilities, he is to that extent bereft of familiar routines or coping strategies. Inevitably the situation is threatening. It was found that many of the incidents

31

and problems raised by the pupils in the course of social education could be related to problems of responsibility and, more specifically, to four crises of responsibility,* as described by Hauser. The relevance of this approach will be apparent from a consideration of each in turn:

a *The 'gate' crisis* – the problem faced by an individual about to cross the threshold into an outside world which he aspires to enter but about which he is apprehensive. An obvious example is the youngster who has been looking forward to leaving school, but then becomes anxious about taking the final step. A more dramatic example would be the long-term prisoner who has been counting the days to his release, and then wantonly commits some act the day before he is due to leave, thus ensuring his continued detention.

b *The family crisis.* The family crisis is perhaps less general than the gate crisis, even though it may well be universal at one stage in life, since it is one aspect of the crisis of adolescence. The discussion, however, centres on the struggle a youngster may have to establish a changed role for himself within the family. Lacking the overnight initiation into adulthood of primitive societies, our children face the problem of achieving their acceptance as adults, having grown accustomed to life within the family as children.

c *The work crisis* – as with the family situation, the youngster faces the problem of establishing himself at work as a fully-fledged worker. Happily, most of the old and often painful practices of 'initiating' youngsters at work have disappeared. However, their one advantage – that the youngster was accepted after his initiation – has disappeared with them.

d *Breakdown.* The problems created by new responsibilities may not always be easily resolved. When they are not, the very fact of failure poses new problems and may lead to a breakdown of those relations which have hitherto sustained the individual in his approach to life as a whole. The breakdown may even extend to other members of the family. Inability to face the prospect of going to work, inability to fulfil one's role expectations within the family group, inability to retain friends and close social contacts, are all aspects of such breakdown. Milder symptoms might be evidenced by frequent job changes or even by increased manifestations of ill-temper.

These themes too may be supported by a variety of media and will be treated in various ways, often including an important element of socio-drama. Such themes as man–woman relationships and the problems of responsibility have a

* This is a short-hand expression which does not necessarily imply a 'crisis' in the usual sense.

wide appeal and a general importance. They are included here because they are clearly a part of social education, and because in the context of the project a variety of approaches was developed specifically to deal with them. Obviously, some teachers may find these approaches useful in the context of general humanities or English courses, without wishing to commit themselves to an overall programme of social education.

5. Identification leading to participation

The final stage in the process of achieving a sense of identification with the community begins with the survey. Surveys enable children to examine particular problems in their life and in doing so to learn a variety of techniques of social interaction, as well as a constructive application of intelligence to social affairs. The occasion for a survey is a decision by the group of children about some action they wish to take, when they have become aware that through group effort they can effect some changes in a situation which they have identified as requiring change.

Before beginning a survey, the group in the class needs to make a hypothesis of its own about the particular situation or problem which they wish to examine in depth. This helps them to recognize their own bias and they can check this initial hypothesis with others which they may develop later. Doing the survey fosters a sense of personal involvement springing from the actual experience of the children. The hypothesis will often arise out of indignation. For instance, one group was convinced of the prevalence of hostile racialist feeling towards immigrants among white children in the school. Testing this hypothesis led to a remarkable concern on the part of a group of children previously untouched by their own work on the area profile.

Once a hypothesis is established, a miniature pre-survey is made to test whether, in broad terms, the main concern is right or wrong. The pre-survey also tests the effectiveness of the tools chosen for the main survey. Thus the group concerned about race relations in the school wanted to use a questionnaire considered tactless by the teacher. They agreed to test it and discuss it with a group of pupils from another school and amended it accordingly. However, the pre-survey may well convince children that their original hypothesis was wrong and nothing needs to be, or can be, done about the problem in question. If they are convinced that they have a case, it is important for the teacher to consider with them the implications of any action which they propose to take. One area survey into the problems of redevelopment started with a concern expressed by some boys in the class about the plans which they had studied. There was

33

concern at particular deficiencies in the proposed services. For instance, the nearest telephone box was a half-mile walk for old people in one new block of flats. This group actually declared that they had stopped 'doing over' phone boxes because they had realized for the first time what the telephone meant to old people.

They also felt concern at adult fatalism about the move out of the area which redevelopment involved for two-thirds of the population. Their area profile had revealed that many people did not want to move and the boys could not see why the plans for land utilization could not be altered to allow for a higher density of population. They wanted the terraced houses rebuilt 'with mod. cons'.

Their concern resulted in four suggestions for action:

1   Refer a case of 'victimization' of an old lady whom they had interviewed to the local councillor.
2   Build up a mobile exhibition for use in launderettes, chip shops and doctors' waiting rooms, which adults were more likely to read and take notice of than the official exhibition set up by the city planning department. Theirs should include estimates of the cost of moving and furnishing a new house, as well as the likely rents. The adults would then see what was involved.
3   Run a poster campaign, based on a cartoon. The cartoon was to depict a family sitting at breakfast ignoring the bulldozer demolishing their wall. The hope was to rouse adults from their sense of fatalism about the re-development scheme.
4   Contribute articles on the implications of the whole redevelopment scheme to a local newspaper.

The concern and involvement shown in the proposed action are an indication of the sense of identification which the process of training in the skills of observation and communication is intended to produce. Just how this happened one cannot say, nor is it easy to say at what point a sense of identification will develop. The only evidence we have is the factual evidence of involvement and the action taken by children. Not all children will become involved at the same time, and individuals may do a number of profiles and other work in social education before their interest develops into a sense of identification with the community sufficient to impel them to take some action on their own initiative.

The last phrase is important. The proposals for action may be the same as those that a teacher would have made much sooner. However, the teacher who accepts the assumption that children should go through a process of social education in order to build a sense of identification will always wait for them to

34

reach their own conclusions about action rather than tell them what they should do. For this is the essential difference between social education at an action level and the concept of community service, in which the teacher may impose his values and his concerns upon the children.

Many teachers will doubtless recognize much of the process we have described, for we do not claim that taken in isolation these suggestions are by any means new. What is new in social education is that it draws together a number of threads which have been developing in good primary and secondary schools often in response to the Newsom and Plowden Reports, and it has inserted some new ideas and some effective techniques. In sum, it provides a more or less systematic perspective for the development and presentation of work in secondary schools.

III. The work of the project: 1969–71

This account describes the work carried out under the auspices of the Social Education Project in the four schools that participated in its second and third years. The chapter is divided into four sections, each of which deals with the work done in one of the schools. Each section opens with a description of the school. The description is not confined to the school itself – its physical characteristics, its organizational structure and its general ethos. It extends beyond the school to the catchment area and the environment as a whole. Such a description is essential, as the environment in which the school is situated must influence the entire social education programme. The environment in which a child is brought up will have an influence upon his needs, and if education is to be concerned with the needs of children, then the environment becomes increasingly important to the teacher. This is even more true of a project in which a major aim is to enable children to become involved in their community. The problems in the area, which the children can be enabled to identify, will have a crucial effect on the final stages, in particular, of a social education programme.

SCHOOL A

School A serves an area which is one of the 'twilight' zones of Nottingham, being due for complete redevelopment during the next few years. Area A, as we will call it, has suffered the same difficulties during recent years as all similar 'running-down' areas in our cities. What was a firmly established working-class area, with many families providing second and third generations of children in the same school, began to change rapidly when it became clear that redevelopment was inevitable. Many of the better-off families moved out and the population became much less stable. The cheap accommodation was sought by poorer families from other areas of the city. The neglect of repairs which would have been carried out in an area with a future, and the dirt and dust of buildings when the demolition period started, added to the problems which beset the area. Those who stayed are people who want to live in Area A when it is rebuilt, some because their family has always lived there, others because they have moved there and like it.

School A was deliberately built outside Area A, in fact it is immediately

across the river from it, in order that the children could have pleasanter surroundings. Housed in fairly modern buildings, which are being enlarged to meet
the needs of the expanding school, are six hundred children who cross the river
each day from Area A to the green surroundings of their school.

School A was one of the three mixed secondary schools in the area when the
project started. One of them, the grammar school, took the children with the
highest attainments. The remainder went to School A or a nearby secondary
modern, according to where they lived. (Those who were nearest to obtaining a
grammar school place formed a 'grammar stream' within School A, which
accounts for the description 'bilateral school'.) However, the first year of the
project coincided with the final year of the secondary modern, which was then
merged, under one headmaster, with School A. The schools operated separately
until the beginning of the third year of the project.

The children are streamed in this school, with the grammar stream at the top
and remedial classes, which are kept deliberately small, at the bottom. The
timetable is organized on a subject basis, although there is a movement in the
school towards the integration of certain subjects, particularly in the humanities.

The organization of the school is not helped by the fact that it is now housed
temporarily in two buildings over a mile apart. The whole issue of discipline
within the school is currently under review. At the time of the inception of the
project, firmness was considered essential. Many of its pupils are 'difficult',
doubtless a reflection of the poverty of their social background and the lack of
stability within the community, as described. Corporal punishment exists,
being exercised at the discretion of the headmaster and senior teachers.

Introductory year: 1968–69
Initially, the work of the project was placed under the direction of a teacher
responsible for much of the remedial work in the school. Two other teachers,
a mathematics teacher and an English teacher, were also involved. Two of these
three teachers observed lessons taken by one of the project team with one class
in each of the second, third and fourth years. Towards the end of the project's
first year they joined in and took some of the lessons, though not always,
consciously, as part of the project. During the first term, these lessons were used
to introduce the children to the idea of observation and communication. Many
of the lessons began as games, with the deliberate intention that the children
should enjoy learning. By encouraging children to observe their classroom, their
friends, school, homes, routes to school and all the other everyday things of life,
it was hoped to draw from them comment and discussion and so to begin the
process of understanding.

37

For the most part, the children concerned had to contend with a long history of failure in school work. Their self-image was damaged and their motivation was low. To counteract these effects it was thought essential to introduce them to a new scale of values. Intellectual competence, as already noted in Chapter II, can be manifested in several ways. The ability to handle abstract ideas is one among several. Social education required a very different kind of competence, i.e. an intuitive social insight and a specifically social intelligence – and here they could begin on an equal footing with any others of their age, regardless of academic 'brightness'. They were shown how important it is to observe things around them and to build up a picture of how these things worked together to shape people's hopes and fears and to impel them to action. This kind of thinking is a supplement to observation, and may be used as a kind of sixth sense, an idea which makes an immediate appeal to children of 12 to 15 years.

The introduction to observation and social understanding was made easier by the use of socio-drama. As there was no tradition of improvised drama within the school, this involved starting at the level of the simplest mime, as described in Chapter II, and progressing to small scenes in which dramatic improvisation was applied to a social content, with the goal of social insight constantly in view.

Of the three teachers who were observing these lessons, one, whose speciality was mathematics, became increasingly interested in the ideas behind the project. He became particularly involved in some work which the children did in a school profile. At this stage of the project, this work was done before a class profile, or any of the simpler profiles, and was not as detailed as the school profiles developed later – indeed, it was not even called a school profile at that time. This teacher found, at this stage, that the project reinforced his own feelings that much school work was irrelevant and ineffective, and he was therefore encouraged to join seriously in the work of the project. At the end of the first year this teacher took over responsibility for co-ordinating the work of the project within the school.

Year 2: 1969–70
During the project's second year, the mathematics teacher, now working with Keith Cordell, took an increasing part in planning the work. Keith Cordell, who was assisting John Rennie, involved four other teachers and attempted to encourage some team-teaching. Although this was only partially successful, two of the teachers retained some interest in the project's work. During this second year, Keith Cordell was working with two classes, one in the third year and one in the fourth year, the latter being the lowest stream in its year. The third-

38

year class had had some experience of social education during the previous year.

The fourth-year class were highly motivated to attempt some work in the near neighbourhood. With this in mind, they built up a survey of the surrounding area. Again, this work was structured less than the area profiles built up later, but the work proved a great help in formulating a structure for area profiles. This project occupied the class for most of the year, since they had only two lessons each week. After completing the survey and presenting the work, they expressed an interest in doing some voluntary work and one or two became involved in this, very much on their own initiative.

The third-year class began by developing the work done during the previous year. Most of their year was taken up with completing a school profile and a profile of a nearby village. These activities had now been developed and structured by the project team in consultation with the teachers, so that the work involved was both more varied and more purposeful than had been the case the previous year. The same class also spent several periods on various aspects of man–woman relationships, using the ideas outlined in Chapter II to extend that section of the third-form curriculum which had hitherto been largely confined to 'sex education'.

Year 3: 1970–71

In the final year of the project, the main effort was concentrated into work with this class, now in their fourth year, most of whom had experienced social education work during the previous two years. Meanwhile, the next-to-the-bottom stream third-year class were engaged on very similar work to that which had been attempted with the third-year class in the previous year. The fourth year, however, undertook a very comprehensive area profile, and as a result of this conducted a survey concerned with the redevelopment of the area. The class evolved a high degree of identification with the community and became involved in a number of small projects concerned with redevelopment.

By now the mathematics teacher was virtually solely responsible for planning the work with Wyn Williams, who had now replaced Keith Cordell. He had become totally committed to the project's ideas, and had contributed valuable papers to the discussions held with teachers from other schools. His enthusiasm was transmitted to several other members of the staff, and three of them became involved in planning a team approach to the work. This was helped by the fact that one had been appointed to act as co-ordinator of an integrated approach to the humanities.

Obviously the most immediate challenges for the social education programme in School A related to the redevelopment plan for Area A due to enter phase one in 1972. Such a situation, affecting the whole environment, human and physical, of the school children, presents exactly the kind of challenge that the social education programme is intended to meet.

It would, however, be misleading to give the impression that the work in this school was geared from the beginning towards an examination of Area A in relation to the redevelopment plans. While this did in fact happen, it happened because this was the way the work developed.

The organization of the school and its underlying assumptions about teacher–pupil relationships necessarily affect the work of the social education programme.

In School A timetabling presented difficulties. While the two periods a week allocated to social education were suitable for the early stages of training in skills, it was not suitable for working on profiles of the school and the area: this kind of work is better dealt with in blocked periods.

There was also a natural concern among subject specialists, in a subject-based timetable, about the possibilities of time being lost to the newcomer in the syllabus. However, the increased interest in integrated studies, reflected by the appointment of the head of curriculum development in the third year of the project, helped to alleviate this problem. In the early stages, the project team were working in an unknown situation – as in all these schools – and the later programmes are a reflection of the recognition by the team, the teachers and the pupils of the most important problems in the communities.

Finally, there was the contrast between the assumptions about teacher–pupil relationships apparent in the disciplinary system of the school and those demonstrated by the project team. In fact, this matter never became serious because the teacher who became most involved in the project work shared the same views about the possibilities of changing the relationship between teacher and pupils.

School B

School B is a girls' bilateral school situated on a large post-war overspill housing estate three miles from Nottingham, separated from the rest of the city by an industrial estate and the river. Once again, the problems which beset Area B are not unique, but are the same as those faced by many council estates. Lacking social amenities, the estate provides little for the youngster. Inevitably, most people look towards Nottingham – an expensive bus ride away – for their leisure. The general uniformity of the buildings on the estate hardly offers the most stimulating environment for the young to grow up in.

All but a few of the boys on the estate go to Nottingham's only comprehensive school. The girls who do not pass for the local grammar school go either to School B or to another bilateral school on the estate. Once again, the buildings are quite modern, the school having been built in 1957, and there are over 650 girls in the school. Like most of the secondary schools on the estate, the school is situated on a perimeter road of the estate, surrounded by pleasant playing-fields.

As one would expect in a girls' school, the social problems of the area are not immediately apparent from the appearance of the pupils. The girls are strongly encouraged to wear school uniform, and very few fail to do so. A premium is placed on quietness and 'good manners'. Whenever the head, deputy head, or a visitor enters a room, the girls stop work and stand as a mark of politeness. The importance of striving to achieve greater success in terms of work, neatness, dress and behaviour is constantly impressed upon the girls. Girls who have achieved success in examinations, behaviour or effort are held up as an example to the rest. Inside the school, it is difficult to realize that Area B has a high delinquency rate and that very many of the girls in this school are 'latch-key' children.

The girls are streamed shortly after they enter the school, the grammar streams forming the first and sometimes the first two streams in each year group. These streams include the majority of the girls who will stay on for examination work in the fifth year, although they are joined by a few others who have shown reasonable promise of some examination success.

The timetable is subject-based, with every subject being taught almost exclusively by specialists. English and mathematics are given major emphasis in the curriculum.

Year 1: 1968–69
During the course of the project, and as part of the work of the project, some of the staff began to plan work as a team and to share responsibility for an area of the curriculum, instead of limiting themselves to their own subject.

During the project's first year, the geography teacher was the only member of staff who had regular contact with the work of the project. She very readily took on most of the teaching herself in the latter part of that year, when the work was mainly concerned with observation and communication techniques, as described in Chapter II. She was also willing to adapt some of her teaching methods in the interests of experimentation, even when they had previously been successful. The class concerned, 2B, finished the year with a class profile.

Year 2: 1969–70

In its second year the project again concentrated on the work of this group, now labelled 3C, and a number of other teachers became involved. Teachers of English, history, RE and art joined in a team-teaching experiment. The first half of the year's work centred on a school profile, followed by a family profile, and the year ended with an area profile.

In the course of their work on the area profile, one group studied emergency services. At one point, members of the fire service were invited to the school for a demonstration and talk, and this prepared the way for a small project on fire prevention. Others were led to undertake work of their own, as well as studying the services around them. Thus, a group studying nursery education began to help in the nursery school, and were encouraged by the teachers to carry this interest further.

Many of the teething problems which most groups of teachers meet when first attempting team-teaching were encountered by these teachers. At one stage some girls remarked, 'We never seem to do anything except social education', an indication of the similarity of approach of the group of teachers. However, by and large these difficulties were overcome, and only staff changes prevented the team from carrying on in the final year of the project.

In addition to this team, a remedial teacher in another class joined in the project and attempted social education work with her own group. However, her interest was not maintained, for she believed that the work was too difficult for her class. By contrast, the project team felt that here the teacher had taken on too much of the work herself, instead of developing the pupils' initiative.

Year 3: 1970–71

In the final year of the project, three teachers, the geography, history and RE teachers, retained their commitment to social education, and only organizational difficulties prevented their working as a team.

The major effort in this final year was with the same class, now 4C, although many of the members of the class had changed during the previous two years. A pattern of work was developed to follow on from their area profiles. This took the form of a local study of the city in terms of new housing developments, a consideration of the social effects of urban renewal, and a survey of the quality of the housing. This programme led on to a study of social problems in the area, including drugs, unmarried mothers, mental health and scapegoatism. Incidental themes created in the course of these studies dealt with social relationships in the family, the neighbourhood and the peer group. The year ended with a study of the problems of starting work. The only involvement in the community shown by the children was a continuation of the small-scale interests developed at the end of their second year.

It should be added that, during the final two years of the project in School B, work was attempted by different teachers with another class in the same year group, but this was on a smaller scale. The challenges of Area B were very different from those of Area A. The greatest challenge lay in the rather unstimulating nature of the environment rather than in any physical deprivation. This affected the way teachers and pupils saw the problems of the estate. There was a keen interest in the difficulties of individuals and the lack of social amenities. This is reflected in the fourth-year syllabus.

Difficulties arose out of the subject emphasis in the school and its concentration on academic success, however limited. The strength of subject specialization presented problems for pupils and staff when asked to tackle work that did not constitute a subject and required an integrated approach. However, although the teachers were not accustomed to team work, great strides were made in this direction. The second difficulty sprang from the school's emphasis on good manners and behaviour. As a result, certain topics were avoided by the staff (thus, the film *Last Bus* could not be shown). Finally, it should be said that the emphasis on encouraging girls to stay on to do examinations resulted in a fairly substantial turnover in the girls involved in social education.

Thus, despite the fact that a consecutive programme was followed by a single class over a period of three years, the benefits to the individual within the class were less marked than might otherwise have been the case.

School C

School C, although in the county of Nottinghamshire, is only three miles from the centre of Nottingham. Views from its windows present a characteristic industrial landscape, with the slag heaps of the nearby pit merging with the hilly outer suburbs of the city. Surrounded by post-war housing, the vast majority of it council-built, the school nevertheless has an interesting 'social mix'. Ten per cent of the pupils are from a predominantly middle-class suburb, until recently still a village. However, the school population is overwhelmingly working class in origin.

Although the policy of the local education authority is towards comprehensivization, the school is a secondary modern, with a catchment area heavily creamed by the nearby grammar school. The buildings and facilities are modern and house 600 boys and girls.

43

Unlike the other three schools, School C is unstreamed. The decision to de-stream was not reached overnight, and was not made solely by the headteacher. Discussion took place over a long period, certainly more than a year, and all the staff were involved. Eventually, a large enough majority of the staff were in favour of de-streaming to make an experimental attempt with the first year. Because of the success of this experiment, a decision was reached to make each succeeding year unstreamed until the whole school became almost completely unstreamed. A division is made at the start of the fourth year when the children who have opted to stay on begin a two-year course leading to the CSE (no GCE is taken), while the non-examination pupils have their own course. Even then, the two groups join together for a considerable part of their timetable.

Each class has a form-teacher who remains with them throughout their time in school. Because of the long-standing stability of the staff, many of the fifth-form pupils have had the same form-teacher since they started school.

There is an ongoing dialogue among the staff which has resulted in a continual development of their programmes in the school. A considerable degree of co-operation exists among the teachers, although they hesitate to call it team-teaching. Nevertheless, as many as six teachers are often involved in planning a series of lessons for a year group. This means that the integration of subjects has had some meaning in School C, and that block-timetabling has resulted in the breaking down of many, if not all, subject barriers.

Within the classroom, a majority of the staff emphasize the value of co-operative learning, and small-group activity is very common in this school. Concomitantly, discipline in the school is very relaxed, and corporal punishment has long since disappeared. Dress and hairstyle are informal, and there is an expectation, on the part of the staff, that children will behave responsibly and be capable of working on their own initiative, even on unsupervised visits outside the school.

Year 2: 1969–70
The second year of the project was the beginning of the involvement of this school in the project's work. Their interest had been expressed during the previous year, and contact had been maintained with the project staff. This led to the beginning of planning during the previous term, which proved invaluable later. Three teachers from the humanities undertook the greater part of the work, although three or four other teachers were involved to a lesser extent. This group remained unchanged throughout the last two years of the project. Planning was the work of the team as a whole, while subsequent execution was left to the individual teacher. Resources were shared and there were frequent discussions

44

about the validity of work attempted. The high level of co-operation between teachers justifies the label 'team-teaching'.

The team approach enabled the whole of the project to extend over whole year groups. During 1969–71, the project team worked with three, and sometimes four, teachers in the second and third year who were teaching within the humanities area of the curriculum (which included English) for two timetabled blocks on one afternoon each. In the initial stages, both year groups spent a considerable amount of time on the basic observation and communication skills, as in the other schools. Both year groups then moved on to class profiles. All this work was planned well in advance at meetings of the teams, and because the beliefs of the staff were so similar to those of the project team no difficulty was encountered in fitting the work into their schemes.

Later, the second-year groups went on to family profiles and finally to school profiles. The third-year groups, on the other hand, went on to school profiles immediately, and then on to area profiles. The project officers were, at first, inclined to resist this as premature. However, the staff had previously begun to develop work in the area, and they had attempted it with the third-year forms. They felt that the time was now ripe and they did not wish to hold off until later. In the event, the area profiles were successful in terms of the interest of the children and the high standard of work produced. Their work on the profile led them to finish the year by studying conservation and pollution. In this, they took the widest definitions of these problems, to include social pollution. The work produced can only be described as outstanding. In fact, the project team, who felt that if anything the teachers had over-prepared the work, had to admit that the end-product justified the method. Instead of leaving the pupils to find examples of their own, the team provided a library of visual aids, and the children were then able to use this material in whatever way seemed most appropriate to them.

Year 3: 1970–71
In the project's final year, the second in School C, the second-year groups followed an identical pattern to that of the previous second-year groups. Different stimuli were used, however, and the content of the work proved, of course, substantially different from that of the previous year. The third-year groups similarly followed the pattern set by their third-year predecessors, in that they worked on area profiles from the start. At the same time, following on from their previous work on the family profile, they turned their attention to 'the generation gap', and this led to some exciting creative work as well as giving plentiful opportunities for socio-drama.

The fourth-year groups began the year with a project called 'Living in Groups' which included a study of three of the kinds of groups described in Chapter II. Basically, this was a consideration of peer-groups, and it formed an extension of the peer-group profile also mentioned in Chapter II. From this sprang a study of 'Outsiders and Scapegoats'. Using the film *I Think They Call Him John* and some extracts from books as stimuli, this study included a look at the causes of scapegoatism, and the jokes which are commonly told against minority groups. A study of 'Law and Order' followed as a logical tailpiece.

Surveys of the area formed the concluding part of their work in a project called 'Needs of Society'. From these surveys, the pupils took the themes 'Leisure' and 'Conservation and Pollution'. Although much of the work of these fourth-year groups and, indeed, the third-year groups involved children going out of school unsupervised to conduct their research, there was no concerted community involvement by the pupils from School C. The only signs were some relatively isolated instances of pupils offering help to old people whom they met during the course of their interviewing. The teachers from School C put this down to their own reluctance to encourage action when the pupils expressed the desire to participate. No difficulties arose from timetabling the work or integrating it with the school programme in School C, and the assumptions and philosophy of the social education team merely reinforced, rather than challenged, those of the school.

School D

Area D is situated about twelve miles outside Nottingham, and has undergone a major change in character during the last fifteen years or so. From being a tiny village, it has been transformed into a much larger community by the discovery of a rich coal seam and the resulting influx of miners. Most of these miners have come from Durham, a few from Scotland and North Yorkshire. Additionally, a small number of professional people have moved in and use the area as a dormitory suburb of Nottingham. It would not have been easy to foresee the difficulties which all these changes have, in fact, brought about. The miners who arrived in the mid-fifties have not integrated socially with the second large influx of miners who came in the mid-sixties. Neither of these groups has integrated socially with the indigenous population. Thus, despite the fact that the 'Geordie' accents of many of the children have been softened by time, and the fact that many of the pupils now in the school were born in Area D, one could sense in the school an undercurrent of the feeling of 'us' and 'them'. This feeling was, however, on the decline during the three years of the project, as the school had worked hard to combat the problem.

46

There is a distinct shortage of employment opportunities in the area and this has had a profound effect upon the school. There is little work, apart from the coal mine, and other jobs must be sought in Nottingham. Working mothers are faced with a long and expensive bus journey, and a number of children have to go home to an empty house. Many school-leavers go into the pit, and an abnormally high percentage into the Services, reflecting the difficulties of the job situation. Again, there is very little entertainment for the young, and children from outlying villages have problems with transport.

The school is part of a modern school complex, within a pleasant campus, where there are three schools: infant, junior and secondary modern – which will become comprehensive under the new plans – with a youth wing attached.

From an organizational point of view, the headmaster has made several experimental changes during the last few years. When the project started, the school was streamed throughout. During the second year of the project, mixed ability groups were tried, but the staff was not happy with this arrangement. 'Banding' has now been introduced, and it appears that this system may remain.

The head has encouraged subject departments to attempt integrated work, and there has been some integration in craft subjects. Discipline in this school is not a problem, perhaps because of the small turnover of staff, and relatively few teachers resort to corporal punishment.

Year 1: 1968–69

The deputy head of the school was the main teacher concerned with the work during the first year of the project, during which time only the more basic observation and communication techniques were attempted.

As in School A, there had been no tradition of improvised drama within the school, and very basic stages had to be gone through. For all three classes concerned, one in each of the second, third and fourth years of the school, the work amounted to little more than an introductory phase of observation and communication, the beginnings of the idea of working together in small groups, and a more participatory kind of atmosphere within the classroom. This seemed even more important than the content of the lessons, since the prevailing methods within the school were far removed from what was considered to be the ideal environment for social education work.

Year 2: 1969–70

At the start of the second year, the deputy head was joined by two other teachers, and more ambitious work was now begun. The deputy head worked with the bottom-stream fourth-year classes, and a general subjects teacher took the bottom-stream third-year classes. These two were helped by a geography teacher, who also did a little social education work with another third-year class. In her work with the third-year class, the general subjects teacher tried to develop the basic work attempted in the previous year by undertaking a class profile. This was done fully and well, and in the course of the programme she was able to extend their work in socio-drama, discussion and presentation. Towards the end of the year, however, some of the work caused problems with the staff of the school. Some of them felt that the challenging and doubting attitudes being encouraged in the social education lessons were damaging to their discipline, as the children wished to adopt the same approach outside social education lessons.

The major part of the work of this group was later taken up with a school profile, and work on relations between the sexes. The latter consisted largely of work undertaken previously by the school, with some additions from the project.

The first half of the year's work in the fourth year was taken up with a large-scale survey of the whole village, which the staff wished to attempt as a previous one had been so successful. The survey involved discovering the facilities available in every house, twelve hundred in all, the information being gathered by interviewing residents in each house. In addition, their feelings about the village were sought. The result was an impressive mass of information, but the children now had very little idea as to how they might collate and use it. Not surprisingly, both teachers and children became disillusioned by this work.

The teachers felt that Keith Cordell ought to take over, and that they themselves should take a less active role. Accordingly, Keith Cordell involved the children in a campus profile, that is a study of all the four schools on the campus. It involved the class in interviewing teachers, including the heads, and children from the other three schools. It led to a suggestion that the school should produce a pamphlet for the benefit of children from junior schools, containing all the details of their school.

Year 3: 1970–71
In the final year of the project, a teacher new to social education joined the two project staff in planning the work of the bottom-stream fourth-year group who were the only group to continue social education work in the final year. Most of the teaching was done by the project staff, although the teacher herself carried out a considerable amount of follow-up work, in between visits from the project staff.

Partly because it was felt that previous work had failed, but also because this class had only a few members who had done social education work before, it

48

was decided that the work should be of a socially remedial nature. With this in mind, the first term's work concentrated on the theme 'Living in Groups', with an emphasis on the children's own peer groups. With help from film, socio-drama, poetry, slides and discussion, the children were led to consider what contribution they could make to group life in various situations, and to understand the causes of behaviour in groups.

In the second term, a very pronounced difficulty in relationships between the boys and the girls in this class led to work on man–woman relationships, and the role of women in society. A small group who were due to leave at Easter split off from the main group and worked on a programme connected with their future careers, including a number of industrial visits. In the final term, this work-orientated approach was extended to the rest of the class, as they too were about to leave at the end of the term. Throughout the year, the emphasis was on oral and creative work, rather than on written work.

Throughout the three years of the project's work in this school, it had to face the problem of fitting an experimental programme into a situation where important organizational changes were already under way. The change from streaming to non-streaming to banding within three years inevitably affected the possibility of retaining a stable group for social education – something the project team considered essential.

This instability undoubtedly affected the cohesiveness of groups. The project team was concerned about this, and felt that much more attention ought to have been paid to it. In a sense, this dictated the syllabus for the fourth year, when no attempt was made to tackle community involvement, but much effort went into getting the pupils to examine their feelings towards one another. At the same time, it must be said that because of the setbacks encountered in the first two years, the teachers were unwilling to continue with the teaching in the third year. They were unhappy about the methods, particularly the use of socio-drama, and they blamed the project team for what they felt was a failure to give direction.

IV. Evaluation

Introduction

The aim of social education is essentially long-term. It is to turn out pupils who as adults will play a fuller part in the affairs of their own community, people who have the sensitivity and the social skills not to be overwhelmed by the complexities of existence in a modern urban environment, people who are willing and able to engage in co-operative activity to help themselves and others towards a wider and fuller mode of social living. One can hope that what was done in a limited number of sessions spread over the quite limited period of one to three years (few of the pupils were continuously involved in the programme) will have contributed something towards these ends. But clearly there is no means of establishing this. Clearly, too, it would be too much to expect that the very tentative re-orientations that were achieved in varying degrees in the few project schools should result in long-term changes which would be clearly discernible in the context of the many other influences which interact in the process of socialization. As any textbook will show,* these include parents, siblings, the community, the peer group, the school, the mass media and indeed the whole gamut of the individual's experience from birth to maturity.

Recent comparative and longitudinal studies† point to the abiding effects of hereditary differences in personality and the importance of early experience.‡

The term 'evaluation' may be used in two senses. The first is comprehensive: to establish the overall value of an enterprise or an institution in some absolute sense. The second is more specific and also more limited: to determine the effectiveness of an enterprise with respect to its own aims. It is not concerned to

* For instance, P. H. Mussen, J. J. Conger, J. Kagan, *Child Development and Personality* (Harper & Row, 1963); W. R. Baller, *Readings in the Psychology of Human Growth and Development* (Holt, Rinehart & Winston, 1962); B. R. McCandless, *Children: Behaviour and Development* (Holt, Rinehart & Winston, 1967).

† For instance, R. A. Levine, 'Cross-cultural study in child psychology', in *Carmichael's Manual of Child Psychology*, ed. P. H. Mussen (Wiley, 1970), Vol. II, pp. 559–612; and N. Bayley and E. S. Schaefer 'Correlations of maternal and child behaviors: data from the Berkeley Growth Study', *Monographs of the Society for Research in Child Development*, Vol. 29, 1964, No. 6 (Whole No. 97).

‡ For an up-to-date and authoritative survey of the many issues raised see *Carmichael's Manual of Child Psychology*, ed. P. H. Mussen (Wiley, 1970), Vol. II.

evaluate these against alternative aims. Nor does it seek to establish the overall value of the institutions in which the enterprise has been pursued. Our attempt in this chapter at evaluating the work of the Social Education Project is strictly limited to this second sense of the term 'evaluation'.

It was realized from the outset of the project that a more limited evaluation should be an essential feature of the work. While it would be impossible to gauge how far the broader and long-term ideals of education have been furthered during the course of our experimental work, it was by no means impossible to assess whether the work appeared to be proceeding on the right lines. For instance, one could ask whether the programmes described in Chapter II did in fact enable those concerned to involve the pupils in fruitful learning experiences. One may ask whether the oral and written work that was produced reached a standard sufficient to give both teachers and pupils a sense of achievement. If the activities themselves were in some sense valid and productive, were they also new and different, or was the entire programme of social education no more than a re-statement of aims and activities which were already features of the school curriculum, albeit under some other name, for example, social studies, humanities, leavers' courses, etc.? Did the pupils enjoy the activities to which they were introduced and did they see them as worth while and relevant to their needs? How far were they themselves able to realize the purpose of social education? Was the impact of the programme sufficient to modify their attitude to school? Finally, since social education aims at the integration of school and community through pupil involvement in community work, did the programme result in any measurable change in the community itself, or at least in attitudes to the schools and their work?

These are the essential questions to which some answers were sought. In addition, attempts were made, although unsuccessfully, to establish (a) whether the pupils had gained anything in social insight and in their own self-image and adjustment, and (b) whether they had learned how to work together more fruitfully in discussing topics of social concern. A list of the techniques adopted and developed as part of this limited evaluation is as follows:

1 teacher interviews;
2 a list of pupils' responses to the concept of social education;
3 interviews with a small but random sample of parents;
4 a test of attitude to school especially developed for the project;
5 a test of children's accuracy in self-perception and peer-perception;
6 evaluation of constructiveness of contributions to group discussion.

Techniques 1, 2 and 3 were undertaken in each of the four project schools, and limited to third- and fourth-year classes who had been involved in the programme. The remaining measures were also given to parallel groups in eight control schools. All evaluation procedures were undertaken during the last twelve months of the project. The single exception was the test of attitude to school, the preparation of which was spread over the period of a year. These procedures are described more fully in the following sections. In each case, results need to be considered separately for the four schools concerned. This is because the direction of the work and also its chief impact proved to be different in each case. As already indicated in Chapter I, the results of our evaluation procedures did in fact agree quite well with the successes and failures of the programme as set out in Chapter III.

Techniques **5** and **6** were less satisfactory. They are included here only for the sake of completeness, and because the procedures themselves may prove a useful starting-point for developing more effective techniques in the future.

Interviews with teachers

There were several reasons for relying on interview rather than questionnaire in attempting to gauge the reactions of teachers to the programme and its implementation. Only a limited number of teachers were involved, thus making it difficult to validate the items in a questionnaire, many of which could have no meaning for a validating control sample. Again, the work involved in the construction of a viable questionnaire would have been out of proportion to the scope of the project. Finally, a questionnaire is necessarily more structured and hence more limiting than a relatively free interview. Precisely because of the importance attached to teacher reaction, it was thought desirable to allow the teachers who had participated to express themselves as freely as possible in relation to the work.

The interviews were conducted in July 1970 by two members of the Diploma Course in Nottingham University School of Education, both experienced teachers who had distinguished themselves by their interest in the work and by their ability to assume an open, acceptant role in the interview situation. Clearly, the results of interviews would have been open to serious criticism had they been conducted by the project workers themselves, or by anyone who had an obvious stake in its success. The interviewers chosen were told to present themselves as neutral fellow-teachers, genuinely anxious to learn from the experience of their interviewees.

The interview itself was freely constructed on the basis of an interview schedule consisting of the following questions:

1 What do you think of the Social Education Project as it affects the pupils?

2   Do you think they have been given too much or too little responsibility?
3   Has it had any effect on the community round about?
4   What has been the effect of the project on the staff of the school as a whole?
5   How much of the work is new?
6   How would you like the work to develop?
7   Should there be more opportunities for exchange of experiences with teachers in other schools engaged in similar work?
8   Has there been enough discussion and planning among teachers concerned within your own school?
9   How can the work be evaluated?
10 Is there anything you would like to add?

Interviewers were free to vary the form of these questions and their order. In addition, supplementary questions were put as necessary to elucidate ambiguities and to enable the respondent to expand in areas which seemed to him to be especially pertinent. All interviews were recorded on tape and transcribed verbatim. The following account is based on the resultant transcription.

School A

Effect of social education on pupils. Of the three teachers interviewed in School A, the first had played a leading role in the work of the project and was strongly committed to its aims. In reply to the first question he referred directly to a statement on aims and evaluation proposed by Lunzer some time previously (see Appendix A2). While pupils had gained in willingness to approach others and to answer questions about themselves, it was not clear that they had gained in the ability to collaborate, to initiate group action and to accept suggestions. Individual differences were very apparent in all these areas, and it was doubtful whether the work of the project had produced any all-round improvement. Self-acceptance and self-understanding were seen by the interviewee as among the principal objectives of his work as a teacher even before the inception of the project. Here, too, he felt that individual differences were so strong as to mask any improvement due to work in social education.

The second interviewee also commented that 'they have learned to talk to people and possibly some go around with their eyes open wider', but added that the work had been too fragmented. To build up new attitudes, it would be essential to begin social education long before the fourth year. The third teacher in this school described the improvement in her own relations with the group concerned, due to a gain in sensitivity, and to the greater interplay among the several ethnic groups involved (the teacher concerned was replying with reference to a second-year group who had been working on a class profile).

Responsibility. Two of the three teachers thought that the fourth-year groups should have been given more help in the preparation of their survey work.

Effect on community. Despite the fact that more time was spent on community survey work in School A than was the case in the remaining schools, all three teachers were agreed that the impact on the community was negligible. One, however, referred to an increased interest in the work of the school by the residents of the adjoining village in which the pupils had been working.

Effect on staff and school. Two of the teachers replied to the effect that the impact on the school as a whole was negligible, and members of the staff who had not been involved had not changed their attitude (in some cases favourable and in others unfavourable). The third interviewee commented on the willingness of staff to give help when asked, but added that they were very sceptical, were not aware of the results of the work and 'tend to draw the worst conclusions about the project as a whole'. The same teacher thought pupils outside the project might be envious of those who had been involved, but she agreed that the project would need to run longer before it had any great impact on the school as a whole.

Novelty of project-based activities. The first teacher commented that, although much of the work was not new, some of the survey work (e.g. of emergency services in the community) *was* new, and the approach was very different, with far greater delegation of responsibility to the pupils themselves. The second interview report echoed these comments. The third teacher noted that while many of the topics might have been touched on incidentally, the project drew them together and gave them a new significance.

Future development. The first interviewee stressed the importance of expecting children to find things out for themselves and giving them more responsibility. He also foresaw the need to find alternative modes of work, since area surveys might be less well received if carried out repeatedly. The second teacher was more despondent, and did not believe that in a mixed community (urban and rural) the work of the school could effect any real integration. The third teacher suggested that much more planning was needed by a team of teachers who were themselves deeply involved in community work.

Discussion. Only this last teacher saw much value in more discussion among teachers within the school, and none saw any great value in exchange between schools.

Summary of School A responses. Each of the three teachers interviewed saw some value in the work of the project and all were agreed on the desirability of (a) a more directed effort on the part of the school to help children to gain an understanding of their community, and (b) more delegation of responsibility to pupils, as was done (perhaps overdone) in the work of the project. However, none of them felt that the work had been going long enough to have made any significant impact on the community or even on the school itself. Two of the teachers referred to the need for greater planning in relation to the future of social education, but one saw this as essentially a team effort, the other as an individual responsibility. In sum, there was a feeling of having participated in a worth-while endeavour, but the sense of achievement in this school was limited and there was a failure to evolve any concrete perspective for further development of the work.

In each school the teacher principally responsible for social education work was given the opportunity of adding a comment to the account of what he had said in 1970, in the light of the experience of the following year. While the staff of Schools B, C and D were happy with what they had already said as a description of the work, the teacher in School A was convinced that the last year of the project was very much more successful.

He noted that pupils who joined the social education group without previous experience of social education rapidly gained in understanding and enthusiasm, mainly from their peers. Social education was contagious. Among the more significant developments, he recorded the fact that several people in the neighbourhood, old age pensioners, community workers and others, were aware of the activities of the youngsters, and approved. At the request of the community worker a group began to work independently on a survey of common interest. Another group carried out a survey of theft in shops, being dissatisfied with the account they had been given by the public. These results were sufficiently interesting in the end for the chief constable to invite them to an interview.

Such was the success of the project that the headteacher commented at the end of the year, 'Even your strongest critics have changed their minds.'

Regrettably, one must conclude on a more sober note. The very next term, new difficulties arose and not all members of staff were as enthusiastic as they had been. Evidently there is still a long way to go.

SCHOOL B

Effect on pupils. The first interviewee stressed pupil enjoyment, but felt that too much had been attempted at once. There had been lack of co-ordination owing to the fact that the timetable was rigidly partitioned into subjects. As a result, members of staff who were interested in social education were apt to undertake similar activities under different headings. Pupils would then comment that they had done this before. The area profile too had suffered from lack of adequate preparation. It was doubtful whether the experience of social education would be apparent when the pupils reached adulthood, but it was possible. Despite the difficulties, the idea of social education seemed sound, and the practice of it appealed to the pupils. The second interviewee replied more briefly, saying that pupils who had some experience of social education were no more 'socially minded' than those who had not. The third interviewee, like the first, commented on the duplication that had been a feature of the work at School B. She would have preferred to see a whole afternoon per week devoted to social education. However, she felt that the pupils were getting 'quite a lot' out of it through getting to know one another and the environment. Pupils in the third year were developing new attitudes. But she was uncertain whether these would not have developed anyway in the fourth year, when some social orientation would have featured in the normal school curriculum.

Responsibility. The first teacher commented to the effect that it was right to give the pupils a great deal of responsibility, but essential to prepare them for it. She illustrated this with a story. A small group of girls in 3C were visiting a health clinic, armed with a questionnaire on teeth. Accordingly they asked one of the sisters how many teeth she took out a day. The sister explained that her work was concerned with eyes and not teeth. The girls' response was simply to repeat the original question. (Of course, if they had simply turned the question into 'How many eyes do you take out a day?' it would still have missed the mark!) More groundwork was essential for work of this kind. Interviews in other schools had been more successful, precisely because the girls were more familiar with the work of schools than that of clinics. The second teacher commented that much of the time the pupils took over, and thought this a good thing. The third re-echoed the experience of the first, commenting that the pupils in the third year might have been better able to cope with the responsibility of area profile work if the ground had been prepared right from the start of their secondary schooling.

Effect on community. There was agreement that the impact on the community had been negligible, apart from those individuals whom the girls had visited or helped.

Effect on staff and school. The first interviewee thought the effect was negligible, as the work was confined to a few classes and a very few teachers. The second indicated that in her experience many of the staff had been approached by pupils in conjunction with the project work, and had expressed a guarded interest. The third felt that the effect had been negative. Their experience of social education work had led some of the girls to be more 'cheeky', and the other teachers were inclined to blame the project.

Novelty of project-based activities. The first interviewee was emphatic that, though much of the work might have featured incidentally in the school curriculum, what was new and important was the sense of direction and the 'streamlined, comprehensive' character of social education in the context of the project. There was a definite programme, as opposed to isolated bits (e.g. old people in the community). The second teacher likewise commented unfavourably on 'the usual do-gooding' undertaken in the fourth year and approved of the fact that social education began in the second year. At the same time, lack of integration occasionally led to work being repeated in successive years. The third teacher (who had previously commented on the way some pupils had irritated some members of staff by their independence) felt that what was most valuable was the co-operation among at least some members of staff, and thought this should be encouraged, e.g. the science teacher should collaborate with others in her approach to sex education.

Future development. During the fourth year, the first respondent said, it was important to begin by a consideration of the group, e.g. the family, and branch out from there. She had seen the programme prepared at School C and was impressed by this. On the other hand, it was important to give the programme to the group, and to be flexible. The second teacher wished to see more work in the community in the last year of the project (the interview was held at the end of the second year). The third stressed the desirability of team work and mentioned the importance of allocating longer periods to social education to enable pupils to do more work outside school.

Discussion. While the second interviewee was lukewarm in her appraisal of the group discussions initiated by the project, both the first and the third were convinced of their importance, the former in particular, stressing the desirability of a 'Committee for Social Education', since the idea of social education was important and would become increasingly so in the next few years.

Summary of School B responses. Two of the teachers (the first and the third) were positively committed to the ideals of the project and were clearly trying to find ways of improving the quality of their work within it. The second interviewee appeared less enthusiastic in her replies, although she was clearly far from hostile. It is apparent that the compartmentalization of the curriculum in School B, and the isolation of the individual teacher, militated strongly against the full implementation of a programme of social education. Nevertheless, there was a clear appreciation of the need to envisage social education as a continuous programme, beginning in the second year if not sooner, with the participation of several teachers in a team. Evidently the pupils enjoyed the work in social education, but without adequate planning there was a danger that gains would be small, and lessons might be repetitive. Independence and pupil direction were seen as positive goals, but the respondent stressed the importance of preparation before letting the children loose on the community at large.

School C

Effect on pupils. One of the teachers interviewed stressed four positive effects: children are encouraged to question standards and attitudes; work in groups, especially in the third year is fostered; education is taken outside the classroom walls; and pupils are encouraged to think what they themselves can do to relieve a social need, even if they cannot do much. The second interviewee was more sceptical, as he felt that the programme put forward as social education was one which in any case informed the work of School C. The third teacher noted that the pupils really enjoyed their work in social education and he put this down to two reasons: the fact that the activities were largely pupil-initiated, and their obvious relevance. He also thought that they had gained new social insights, *particularly* in relation to their own reactions as individuals in changing groups, although he conceded that this was no more than an impression.

Responsibility. The first reply was that it was right to give pupils responsibility. In any case School C encouraged pupils to work independently outside the confines of the school precincts. Interviews in other schools had been especially revealing. On occasions, however, pupils were liable to upset some interviewees, e.g. traditionally-minded teachers, by the directness of their approach. The second teacher again replied more briefly, commenting that, even when pupils had spent a whole afternoon on their own carrying out an assignment outside school, the majority had 'lapped it up' and only a few had 'larked about'. The third replied in much the same way. Even in the second year, pupils had gone out of school, e.g. to visit old people, whereas this would normally have been postponed to the fourth year. It was important that pupils be given the opportunity to 'skive and not work'. Only one or two availed themselves of it. The fact that they organized their own groupings was also important.

Effect on staff. Two of the interviewees felt that the effect on staff was negligible. There were some who favoured social education and others who were sceptical, but these attitudes existed before the project and had not altered significantly. The third insisted that the ideas underlying social education were accepted by the entire staff. To begin with, however, there had been poor organization and some members of staff had opted out, while others were sufficiently committed to get down to the construction of actual syllabuses and themes, and to their implementation in the classroom.

58

Effect on community. There was general agreement that the project had made no impact on the community in general. One interviewee referred to the fact that some householders were irritated by the questions they were asked, although others, especially the old, seemed gratified. The same teacher felt that interviews and survey work in general should in future be followed up, so that some good might come out of it.

Novelty of project-based activities. Again the replies were along similar lines. In a general sense, social education had been a feature of the work of the school before it became associated with the project, partly through work on a humanities programme. On the other hand, topics were treated in a different way in the light of the new conceptions, and the experiment seemed justified. Examples were the discussion of the immigrant issue as an illustration of a more general problem of scapegoats and outsiders; or the consideration of a topic such as the treatment of the criminal by inviting prison officers to the school and putting questions to them instead of obtaining material from books; or the use of the class and school profile. In general, it was recognized that the social education programme fostered a direct approach to problems by finding things out at first hand, rather than the indirect approach which was characteristic of most interdisciplinary curricula, and this was held to be a good thing.

Future development. All three interviewees were convinced of the validity of social education, at least for schools which were willing to accept it. Two of the teachers spoke of the effort required of the individual member of staff, and stressed that, because of these demands, there was a need for contact between schools, or it would be too easy to allow the work to lapse. The third suggested that social education could be approached in at least three ways: one was as a distinct subject, and this might be particularly appropriate for schools which stressed a structured timetable; another was to integrate the conceptions and approach of social education with a humanities scheme, as was being done at School C; the third was the implicit approach via the school ethos.

Discussion. The first interviewee was emphatic about the need for better communication within the school. He believed that the project had got off to a bad start in School C, due to insufficient direction or at least to insufficient planning: 'teachers, whatever their failings, like to feel that something is going to happen and it does happen, not that it might happen'. It was essential that the whole staff should know in advance what is being planned. The third interviewee also felt that many of the teachers in School C had opted out owing to a failure of communication between teachers who were involved in the project and those who were not. He also saw value in meetings with teachers in other schools. The second interviewee, however, was satisfied that informal discussion

59

among the teachers most concerned was all that was needed, and this had been a very positive feature of their work.

Summary of School C responses. The very fullness and constructive nature of replies given by teachers in this school may be taken as an indication of their commitment to the ideas of social education. Nevertheless, it was apparent that the work of the project had not made much impression on teachers not directly associated with it. Despite the fact that similar lines of endeavour had been pursued before the inception of the project – or perhaps because of it – the teachers in this school were convinced of its novelty and of the positive contribution that it made. In this connexion, they stressed the continuous character of the work from the second year onwards. In addition, they had been encouraged to allow pupils a very considerable degree of responsibility and freedom, and they were pleased with the results. One might paraphrase the comments by saying that giving children freedom is a necessary precondition for the development of responsibility. Only in isolated instances did the pupils fail to profit. Two of the teachers were emphatic about the need for planning. It is clear that initially the emphasis on self-direction had made for an excessively hand-to-mouth approach, but these weaknesses were corrected as the project continued. The extension of the work to the community was seen as important, and even crucial, and in this connexion it was stressed that the onus was partly on the teacher to be involved in the community and its affairs in order to foster a climate within which constructive suggestions would come forward and could be implemented.

SCHOOL D

Effect on pupils. Of two teachers interviewed one commented that pupils enjoyed the lessons with the project workers (not commenting on her own work) and had picked up some of the points, but they seemed unable to relate what they had learned to the rest of their work in school. The second interviewee commented on the unevenness of pupil response to her own work. She did not see any real change in attitude and was very doubtful about what children might get from social education in the long run.

Responsibility. Both team teachers commented on disciplinary problems stemming from the contrast between the relaxed discipline and demand for maturity made by social education and the general ethos of the school.

Effect on community. Neither interviewee was of the opinion that there had been any positive impact on the community. One commented that while people in the village which the pupils had visited were glad of the interest shown to begin with, they tended to treat subsequent visits as importunate.

60

Effect on staff and school. It was apparent from both interviews that for the most part the staff were hostile to the work of the project, and blamed it for behavioural problems encountered outside its sphere.

Novelty of project-based activities. The first respondent replied that the topics were new as matter to be taught in schools. The second commented that some of the techniques were new, and referred in particular to socio-drama. She thought that not every member of staff could cope with this approach. She also believed that the techniques used in social education might have been more successful with pupils of higher ability.

Future development. The first teacher replied that 'if social education is going to be adopted at all, it should be throughout the whole school', not as one subject but throughout all subjects. The second also felt that it was wrong to put social education as a subject on the timetable. But she felt that in so far as the aim was to build an attitude of mind, she had been more successful in doing this with the kind of work she had been doing before.

Summary of School D responses. The pupils had apparently failed to gain a great deal from the activities in social education. Pupil response had been uneven, and staff response had been negative. Although the approach of social education was seen as new, it was not seen as universally applicable, since too much depended on the special abilities of the teachers and the general ability of the pupils concerned. The only hope for its implementation lay in the conversion of the school as a whole, so that all its work is informed by the ideas of social education.

Comments

In the above account, we have on occasion used the form 'the respondents were agreed . . .' This is no more than a stylistic convenience and it is stressed that each interview was independent. On the other hand, it is clear that, within each of the four schools, the replies given by the several teachers involved do show a large measure of agreement. Doubtless, this is in part a reflection of the frequency of informal discussions within the school among teachers who participated in the project. This is in strong contrast to the lack of communication between staff engaged on the project and the remainder of the school staff. Several of the interviewees referred to this failure, and it is apparent that in School D as well as, to some extent, in School B the reactions of some members of staff became or remained negative.

Clearly, the experiences of the project differed fairly widely from one school to another. Nevertheless, it is possible to discern a number of points of convergence. To begin with, with the partial exception of School D, there are references to pupil enjoyment of social education work in every group of interviews. More-over, all the interviewees accept its relevance, and several refer to the pupils' recognition of the relevance of the work. In one way or another, there is agree-ment that whether or not the topics are new (they were new to some teachers and not to others), the methods were different, in particular because of the reliance on a more direct approach in obtaining information, and because of the emphasis on freedom and responsibility for the pupils. In three of the schools, second- or third-year pupils were sent out into the neighbourhood on their own to find things out, where previously such an arrangement might have been regarded as a daring enterprise to be risked once or twice with fourth-year leavers, and another difference in method was the progressive developmental programme envisaged by social education (class profile, school profile, neighbourhood survey, community involvement).

There is also some agreement on the negative side. Inadequate structuring of the programme is referred to by teachers in School C, while one of the inter-viewees in School B referred to the (later) work of School C as an example to other schools of the careful planning that was needed. Clearly, there is a problem in achieving a satisfactory equilibrium between the need to promote pupil initiative (to work from the ideas expressed by the pupils themselves, to gear the work to the particular interests and abilities of the group concerned – see, for example, comments about School B), and the need to provide an adequate perspective for pupils and especially for the teachers (cf. the comments quoted verbatim from the first respondent in School C). This is a problem to which we will return in Chapter VI.

Again, one may note that in more than one school there were comments that pupils had gone out to conduct interviews with insufficient preparation. In point of fact, this was particularly true in School D (see Chapter III), and it was largely due to this that the project there was unsuccessful. One of the respondents in School D commented that while initially a display of interest by the school in the community might be welcomed, repeated visits would rapidly lead to indifference and even hostility. It is clear that the teacher in School C who referred to the need for an active involvement in the community by at least some teachers as well as by the pupils had this problem very much in mind. This problem too is one that will be taken up again in Chapter VI.

At this point it is appropriate to make the following observation. The aim of social education is to foster an informed interest and involvement in community affairs, but in no way to train pupils in techniques of quantitative social analysis. To carry out a large-scale house-to-house survey, posing very general, perhaps superficial and sometimes personal questions (as was done at School D), is at

62

best to kill the goose that lays the golden egg: assuming the project to be successful when it is done the first time, what remains to be done the next year, and the year after that? If, however, the aim is seen as one of acquiring commitment and involvement, then a wide and varied perspective is immediately opened up. Interviews at the door cease to be seen as the only means of achieving the end, but only as one method among many (cf. the examples cited by the teachers themselves of bringing the interviewee to the school). Nor are they ever to be introduced as the initial step in an inquiry. Their purpose is to provide a dimension of reality and a first-hand interaction between the pupil and the interviewee, and not to produce a statistically reliable breakdown of some set of variables in the community as a whole. The character of the work can change from year to year, reflecting changes in the interests of the groups concerned, as well as changes in the immediacy of specific problems in their community (for example, redevelopment, waste disposal, road safety, playground facilities, welfare for the old, etc.).

Finally, several of the interviewees referred to the clash between the relaxed discipline required by social education and the more rigorous standards that may be upheld in any school to which it is introduced. Again, the problem is real. Social education does demand a more or less fundamental change in teacher–pupil and school–pupil relations. It is intended as education towards responsibility and it is actively opposed to anything that smacks of child-minding or child obedience training. While it is true that no reasonably well run school can be consciously committed to the latter aims, one may ask whether they are not the ends that are sought unconsciously and unreflectively through the paternalistic discipline which is characteristic of many schools. If this is true, then the problems are indeed inescapable, and Chapter V includes a number of vivid examples of how they were manifested. Once more, the clash was most acute in School D, and the respondents – three sheep in a herd of goats – were inclined to give up: social education was all very well provided it permeated the whole school in all its activities. The implication is *non nobis*. The very real, if limited, progress displayed in Schools A and B testifies against this counsel of despair. While some staff were sceptical or even hostile, others were intrigued and even envious. Moreover, the comments from School C, which did indeed conform in some degree to the desired image, indicate that a common purpose is not enough. Much work needs to be done and many mistakes will be made before it can be said that social education in any school is an unqualified success.

With regard to the last question put to the interviewees, there is little need to itemize replies. None of them felt that evaluation was possible in any important sense, though all agreed that it was at least an administrative necessity. The proof of the pudding is in the eating, and the reader must be judge.

Pupil attitude to social education

A measure of attitude to social education was obtained from pupils in each of the four schools during the spring of 1971. For this purpose it was decided to invite written responses to open-ended questions, rather than offer a multiple-item questionnaire. The latter technique, which was used in the measurement of attitude to school, was in fact precluded for the present purpose, since there was no reference group upon which to validate the form of the questionnaire. The group of pupils to whom the questions were directed was the only group who had experienced social education over a period, and this group was, of course, quite small. In Schools A, B and C, the questions were put to third- and fourth-year pupils, while in School D only the fourth-year group participated, since this was the only class then involved in the work of the project. In all cases the survey was confined to pupils who had experienced social education over a period of at least five years. Thus the total number of respondents was 79.

The questions on attitude to social education were put by two helpers, unknown to the pupils and teachers, and otherwise not actively connected with the project.* Only two questions were asked, and these were put to the groups orally. The first was a request for a definition of social education: 'What is social education? Write down in your own words what you think social education is. You have your paper, and you can write as much or as little as you like, just so you explain what social education is.' The second question requested a statement of attitude: 'Do you like social education or not? If you like it, then say why you like it. If you don't like it, then say why you don't. You can put these answers any way you like. If you have a lot to say, your answer will be long, and if you have little to say it will be short. Either way is all right, so long as you put down what you really think.' The students were told not to put their names on these papers and were assured that their answers would not be shown to members of staff within the school – who would, of course, have been able to identify each respondent by his handwriting.

The replies to the first question usually extended to a short paragraph rather than a single sentence or phrase. Not infrequently there was some redundancy in what the children offered, the same information being repeated in different words. Nevertheless, it was found possible (a) to pick out within each response sheet one or more ideas, and (b) to categorize these according to type. Seven such categories were found by examination of the replies. The seven categories

* As in other parts of the evaluation, the helpers were teachers on secondment for a diploma course within the School of Education.

were arrived at after careful examination of all the replies by a team of four judges. They were:

i learning about the environment, e.g. 'Social education is finding out about things outside school, about how people live, studying our school and our homes' (School A);

ii learning to understand people, e.g. 'Social education is finding out about other people and what they are like' (School B);

iii definition in terms of work done on the project, e.g. 'It is a subject in which we do things. For instance, interviewing people, visiting, drama . . . talking about how bad things are and finding out things' (School B);

iv reference to pupil participation, e.g. 'A new form of education in which pupils' views count a lot more than they used to and they have a lot more say in what they do' (School C);

v reference to pupil enjoyment;

vi reference to pupil responsibility and relation to maturity, e.g. 'It is when you go around in an adult way, acting like an adult' (School A);

vii reference to specific lessons, e.g. 'Social education is when you have a long discussion between boys and girls about work for instance' (School D).

Table 1 shows the distribution of responses according to the number of categories they record.

Table 1 Distribution of responses by number of underlying categories

School	0	1	2 or more	n
A	2	17	8	27
B	0	10	5	15
C	0	12	10	22
D	0	14	1	15
All	2	53	24	79

Several pupils offered ideas included in more than one category, e.g. 'A form of teaching whereby you teach yourself' (Category **vi**). 'You go out to places and get information and then you put it down on paper and exhibit it to show people things they would not usually find out' (Category **i**). (School A.)

The uncategorized replies were from two very retarded pupils whose scripts proved too brief to interpret. The number of categories mentioned by the respondents is some indication of the fullness of their replies. To some degree it reflects their appreciation of the many-sidedness of social education. This is offset by the effect of scholastic retardation. Nevertheless, it is interesting to note that in School C, where both the project workers and the teachers concerned (see previous section) were most happy about the course of the work, nearly half the pupils offer complex replies, while in School D, where the teachers as well as the project workers were least satisfied, only one pupil out of fifteen does so. The remaining schools fall between these two.

Table 2 shows the distribution of categories by schools. Because of the responses in the third column of Table 1, n rises to 99.

Table 2 Distribution of response categories

School	i	ii	iii	Category iv	v	vi	vii	Total
A	8	9	1	4	2	6	0	30
B	7	7	1	0	1	0	4	20
C	15	6	10	1	1	0	0	33
D	1	3	1	0	0	1	10	16
Total	31	25	13	5	4	7	14	99

Comparing these distributions, it is apparent that the majority of Category **vi** responses are made by pupils in School A. The following example appears to illustrate what some of these pupils are struggling to express, although few are so eloquent:

> Social education is a different form of education which reaches the pupil deeply. It gets to them in a way which triggers off something inside and helps you and makes you work as though you are the only teacher to tell yourself what to do in which more progress comes from you. Then you are pleased with yourself and this gives you more and more confidence in yourself. At that point social education has made you.

It seems likely that this kind of reaction, however expressed, indicates a response to the deeper involvement in community affairs that was realized in School A. At the same time, the measure of self-direction allowed in the course of project work, especially in the last year, was in some contrast to the more traditional climate generally prevalent within the school.

Comments from School B seem to show an awareness of the purpose of social education, but there is little indication that the imagination of the girls has been fired. The following are examples:

> Social education is a project on all subjects in school, e.g. we do about Nottingham, then old, young and middle-aged people. Drama is added to this. Besides this we do about drugs, smoking, letters of complaint, mentally handicapped people. S.E. is social work, doing things in the outside world. (Category iii)

> We do things to help people and to find out what kind of a world we live in. (Category i)

In School C, the same overall understanding is apparent, but the involvement appears to be deeper, and there is greater maturity in the mode of expression as well as in the appreciation of the purpose of the work.

> Gives a wider scope of imagination, understanding people and looking about you . . . is dedicated to the social needs of the community and environment in general. (Category ii)

> Finding out for yourself about the environment we live in, about the schools in the district, how they teach the children, do they believe in streaming, should the 11-plus be abolished, pollution, how the world is slowly being poisoned, how we can stop it, how a law court works, etc. (Category i)

Perhaps the sharpest contrast in Table 2 is that between the other three schools and School D, where the concentration of replies in Category vii (definition by enumeration of one or more specific lessons) suggests that the pupils have failed to see an overall purpose in the work. During the final year in School D, the work in social education was closely controlled and largely executed by the full-time project workers. Nevertheless, the impact of this effort was apparently less than it was in other schools, and this may well be due to lack of continuity. One of the points that has been stressed throughout this report is the importance of viewing social education as a continuous process which must begin early in the secondary school if the aims are to be fully realized by the time the pupil reaches the end of his schooling.

The preceding examples have deliberately fastened on differences between schools. It is important to do this, since the circumstances of any given school cannot but affect the way in which social education is introduced and adapted. However, it is equally important to recall that the similarities in Table 2, reflecting similarities in the responses themselves, outweigh the differences. In three of the four schools, the majority of the pupils spontaneously define

67

social education by reference to one or other of its major aims (learning about the environment, Category **i**, learning about people, Category **ii**) or by discussing the broad areas of activity through which these are realized (Category **iii**). An examination of replies to the second question ('Do you like social education; why or why not?') shows that this widespread appreciation was accompanied by favourable attitudes which were even more widespread, since these extended to all four of the project schools.

Table 3 Favourable and unfavourable attitudes to social education

School	Favourable	Unfavourable	Neutral	n
A	21	3	3	27
B	14	1	0	15
C	19	0	3	22
D	10	3	2	15
All	64	7	8	79

The distribution of attitudes in Table 3 is striking, when it is recalled that these responses were drawn from senior pupils in the lowest streams of the secondary school, that respondents were encouraged to state their opinions freely, that the teachers were themselves neutral, being neither teachers within the schools nor members of the project staff, and that anonymity was 'guaranteed' (and preserved).

Reasons given for liking social education fall into three groups. The first is the inherent interest and variety of the work:

> I like S.E. because it is interesting and we found out a lot. We do different things each time and not the same things all the time. (School A)

> I like S.E. very much because these lessons are very much different from others because we do all kinds of different things and not one thing all the time. (School A)

> I like S.E. because it is interesting. It is the only lesson that we can get together and talk serious – everybody joins in the discussion. (School D)

> I like it because you can go out of the classroom and find things out for yourself instead of sitting behind a desk and writing from a book – which is very boring. It is much more interesting to work in this way because as you

learn to go out and explore, you learn to communicate with people much better. (School C)

In the second group, the emphasis is on the relevance of social education, especially to vocational preparation and preparation for citizenship:

I like S.E. because I think it helps me a lot about people and work. We learn to help people. (School A)

I like S.E. because it teaches you to be quicker to what people are saying to you. It matures you ready for when you leave school or college. It teaches you to understand what goes on around you as the world changes. It broadens your mind. It gives you a chance to do what you want to do. (School C)

It gives you the chance to get out and about. You learn things and hear things and see things that you have never heard before. It also gives you the chance of achieving something and being part of something. It gives you also something to look forward to. (School C)

The two examples from School C again illustrate the maturity of outlook achieved by the adolescents in this group. Each incorporates a reference to personal growth. There is, however, a small group of responses in which the gain in personal adequacy is central:

I like it first because it is a different kind of work instead of writing and doing what the teacher tells you to do. Another reason is because you are treated more like a grown-up. The next reason I like it is because you gain self-confidence and you are able to mix with different people. (School A)

I like S.E. because before this started I was afraid to talk to some people and agree or disagree with them. (School A)

As is apparent from Table 3, expressions of dislike were rare in any school. The reasons that were offered do not help as much as they would had they pinpointed aspects of the work which made no appeal to pupils in general, but which had been glossed over by other respondents. In fact, they simply focused on the same aspects as the positive responses, with a contrary evaluation:

I dislike S.E. I don't think you should discuss anything about anybody else. (School D)

It seems silly, but I don't like S.E. because the teacher does not help you and you are able to go through the day aimlessly. (School A)

I dislike S.E. for one reason, that it's boring. (School B)

Comment

Taken overall, the responses given by these pupils are in some contrast to those given by their teachers. The latter, as we saw, were often tentative, and general approval was moderated by expressions of caution, especially in relation to the novelty of the project, the generality of its impact and even its appropriateness for the group of pupils concerned. The replies of the children are overwhelmingly favourable. In three of the four schools the qualitative breakdown of replies strongly supports a judgement that the children not only enjoyed the work but that they correctly appreciated its aims and their relevance.

It is tempting to write off the near unanimity of these reactions by ascribing it to a 'Hawthorne effect'.* There is no doubt that almost any new project can expect to meet with an initial and spurious success which is simply due to its novelty. In the present case such a judgement is probably misleading. The Social Education Project differs from the majority of experiments in innovation precisely by its failure to provide an impressive array of new materials and instructions for using them. The novelty that it provides is built into the work itself and is therefore self-perpetuating. For throughout its operation the project workers emphasized the importance of ensuring that the details of its implementation must not be laid down in advance, but should be left to the co-operative decision of the group itself (guided by the teacher). It will be recalled that in the classic Hawthorne experiment repeated increases in productivity were due not merely to the novelty of the measures introduced by the management, but to the fact that these were introduced in response to the requests of the operatives. Thus this evidence also supports the view that improvement in morale results from the achievement of a genuine sense of participation rather than from a novelty effect per se.

Attitude to school

As indicated earlier, in measuring attitude to school it was possible to use a more objective instrument. Among existing measures, particular attention was given to a questionnaire by Fitt† and to the questionnaire for primary-school pupils devised by Barker-Lunn for the NFER.‡ In the event, it was decided not to use

* See G. C. Homans, 'Group factors in worker productivity' reprinted in *Readings in Social Psychology*, ed. E. E. Maudsy, T. M. Newsoms and E. L. Hartley (Methuen, 3rd edn, 1958).

† A. B. Fitt, 'An experimental study of children's attitudes to school in Auckland, New Zealand', *British Journal of Educational Psychology*, Vol. 26 (1956), 25–33.

‡ J. C. Barker-Lunn, *Streaming in the Primary School* (NFER, 1970).

either, on the grounds that the first is short and may not adequately reflect the many facets of pupil attitude in relation to school, while the second, although excellent in this last respect, is designed specifically for primary-school pupils, so that the items are not always the most appropriate in an inquiry aimed at teen-agers. However, in the selections of items for a new and purpose-built measure of school attitude, the Fitt and especially the NFER scale were found to be most valuable points of reference.

Before discussing how the scale was used in the evaluation of the project, something must be said about its construction. This was inevitably somewhat hurried in view of other demands made on members of the team, but neverthe-less included the three control phases: item selection, preparation and analysis of a try-out scale, and administration of a final scale.

In selecting items for the try-out scale, some use was made of three sources. The first consisted of the published scales of Fitt and Barker-Lunn; the second was an open-ended test given to classes of children in two of the project schools (Schools C and B); the last was the writers' experience which was used in supply-ing gaps in the requirements after compiling a possible scale based on the other two sources. The open-ended test was simply a request to pupils in the classes concerned to complete the sentence 'School is . . .' In the event, by selecting key phrases from among the answers provided by these boys and girls, it was found possible to devise a considerable number of relevant items, in the confident anticipation that they would discriminate in a secondary-school population.

Pooling together all three sources, a try-out scale was constructed comprising ten items under each of the headings: attitude to school, attitude to teacher, attitude to pupils, conformity (attitude to rules) and self-concept, making a total of fifty items. This scale was administered to a sample of two hundred children in a comprehensive school unconnected with the project using the standard Likert procedure – i.e. a tick was required for each item in one of five positions representing a scale from 'strongly agree' through 'uncertain' to 'strongly disagree'.*

Results from this try-out were then used to refine the scale and to shorten it. Intercorrelations between the fifty items were calculated and the resultant matrix was analysed, using the method of principal components followed by rotation to the Varimax criterion, all calculations being done on the Nottingham University KDF 9 computer.

The factor pattern obtained from the factor analysis differed substantially from the original five sub-scales. Interpretation of the most significant factors

* See for example A. N. Oppenheim, *Questionnaire Design and Attitude Measurement* (Heinemann, 1966).

suggested six usable scales, with an overall attitude to school based on the test as a whole.

In designing the final scale, a number of items were dropped because their interpretation was clearly ambiguous, while others were found to be redundant, since the relevant scales were well covered by other items. The final scale used in the evaluation consists of thirty items and is reproduced in Appendix C. The sample used in the evaluation was considerably larger, the test being completed by social education groups in each of the four project schools and by parallel classes in a further eight schools used as a control group, with a total sample (n) of 530.

The intention in selecting control schools was to match each of the project schools with two non-project schools similar in their organization and in the catchment area upon which they draw. For purposes of data analysis, project and control schools were allocated numbers from 1 to 12 and the latter will be referred to by these numbers throughout the chapter. Numbering of project schools and associated controls was:

Project schools	Associated control schools
A (10)	11, 12
B (3)	1, 8
C (9)	2, 5
D (7)	4, 6

Unlike the expression of attitude to social education, measures of attitude to school afford only a very indirect estimate of the effectiveness of the social education programme, which occupied only a small part of the work of the school. Such attitudes can be expected to reflect a great many factors both inside and outside the schools. Nevertheless, it was hoped that the introduction of the social education programme would tend to make more pupils feel that school is a place where worth-while activities are pursued.

Since the attitude scale was administered to third and fourth forms in all twelve schools (in the eight control schools the classes chosen were those which most nearly paralleled the associated project classes, i.e. one or two of the lower stream classes), the results were analysed separately for the two year groups.

Figure 1 shows the relative mean scores for each of the eleven schools (third-year pupils) and for the twelve schools (fourth-year pupils).

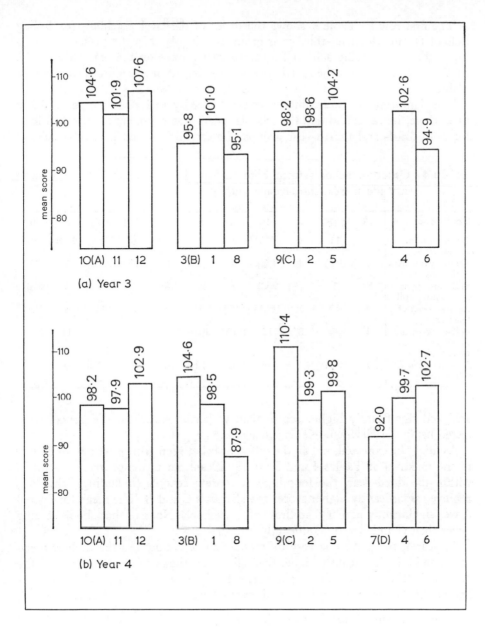

Fig 1. Attitude to school

The first row in Table 4 shows the order of the twelve schools (excluding School D, in which no third-year group was involved in the project) according to the mean scoring achieved by third-year groups on the scale as a whole. Similarly the results for the fourth-year groups are summarized in the first row of Table 5.

The significance of these differences was tested by analysis of variance. Taken as a whole, it was found that the schools' effect was significant at the 0·01 level for both third- and fourth-year groups. To establish which particular schools

Table 4 Order of schools from high to low (left to right) based on mean attitude scores (third-year groups)

Total scale	12	10(A)	5	4	11	1	2	9(C)	3(B)	8	6
Acceptance of school ethos	12	11	4	10(A)	2	1	3(B)	6	5	9(C)	8
Friendly relations with class	1	3(B)	4	9(C)	5	8	6	12	10(A)	2	11
Self-concept as successful pupil	12	1	10(A)	9(C)	2	11	8	4	5	6	3(B)
Appreciation of teacher	4	12	5	10(A)	9(C)	1	2	6	11	8	3(B)
Self-concept as socially acceptable	1	4	8	12	10(A)	3(B)	5	6	2	11	9(C)
Absence of low self-concept	1	10(A)	5	6	9(C)	12	8	2	3(B)	4	11

achieved significantly higher scores than which others, these differences were tested using the Newman–Keuls procedure.*

As might be expected, not all the differences between groups which contribute to the rankings of Tables 4 and 5 are significant. In terms of overall attitude, within the third year, the four highest scoring schools (including School A) achieved significantly higher scores than Schools C and B. The mean for School A was significantly higher than those of five schools. None of the schools scoring lower than C and B was significantly lower.

At year 4, the picture is very different. School C now has the highest mean score, and it is significantly higher than all of the other schools. School B has the next highest score, significantly superior to eight other schools. On the other hand School A, in ninth rank, is significantly lower than three others (Schools C,

* See B. J. Winer, *Statistical Principles in Experimental Design* (McGraw-Hill, 2nd edn, 1971).

74

B and 12), while School D (not included in Table 4) is significantly lower than nine others.

It would be foolish to exaggerate the implications of these findings. The very fact of the wide differences in scores achieved by third- and fourth-year groups in some schools, notably Schools A, B and C, is proof enough that the test cannot be taken as an overall measure of the schools' success in motivating pupils

Table 5 Order of schools from high to low (left to right) based on mean attitude scores (fourth-year groups)

Total scale	9(C)	3(B)	12	6	5	4	2	1	10(A)	11	7(D)	8
Acceptance of school ethos	12	3(B)	9(C)	1	6	2	10(A)	4	7(D)	11	5	8
Friendly relations with class	5	3(B)	4	6	9(C)	11	2	12	8	1	10(A)	7(D)
Self-concept as successful pupil	9(C)	12	11	4	10(A)	6	1	2	5	3(B)	7(D)	8
Appreciation of teacher	9(C)	12	4	3(B)	5	11	6	1	10(A)	2	7(D)	8
Self-concept as socially acceptable	11	9(C)	5	2	3(B)	1	6	4	12	8	10(A)	7(D)
Absence of low self-concept	6	10(A)	9(C)	11	12	2	1	5	4	3	7(D)	8

in their lower streams. On the other hand, the relatively favourable attitudes of the fourth-year groups in two of the project schools may well be a pointer to the effectiveness of the programme in combating a fairly widespread tendency among these groups (the lowest streams) to see school as increasingly irrelevant to their needs. Thus in only one other school (School 6) did the fourth-year group achieve a significantly higher mean score than the corresponding third-year group, while significant differences in the opposite direction were found in four schools (although one was School A).

To obtain a clearer picture of what the test measured, inter-item correlations were again calculated for all 530 subjects who had completed the final thirty-item test, and the resultant matrix was again examined by factor analysis. Significant loadings for the Varimax rotation are shown in the table in Appendix C, pages 158–9. The factor pattern closely resembles that obtained from the try-out test, and this was used as the basis for the determination of six sub-scales.

The following is a list of these, together with an illustrative item for each:

1. Acceptance of school ethos, e.g.
   I like to get on with my work quietly.

2. Friendly relations with class, e.g.
   I would like to get away from children in my class. (Answered negatively.)
3. Self-concept as successful pupil, e.g.
   I think I am pretty good at school work.
4. Appreciation of teacher, e.g.
   The teacher helps the slow ones in a nice way.
5. Self-concept as socially acceptable, e.g.
   I think people like working with me.
6. Sense of personal adequacy (absence of self-punishment), e.g.
   When I have a row with my friends it is usually my fault. (Answered negatively.)

The procedure for calculating sub-scale scores is given in Appendix C (see page 158). Such sub-scale scores were obtained for all of the 530 pupils in the inquiry and the results were examined for differences between schools, following the same statistical procedure as that used for the overall attitude scale. Rank orders of schools for the separate sub-scales appear in the lower portion of Tables 4 and 5 for third-year and fourth-year groups respectively.

Again, differences between schools are not always significant. In the third forms, School 12 obtained a significantly higher score than Schools B and C (among others) for sub-scale 1, and School 11 scored significantly above School C (but not B). Differences for sub-scales 2 and 6 were not significant. For sub-scale 3, School B scored significantly lower than four other schools, including School C – doubtless reflecting the stress on academic achievement in School B noted in Chapter III. Similarly, for sub-scale 4, the five lowest ranking schools, including School B, obtained significantly lower scores than the three highest ranking schools. For sub-scale 5, only one difference was significant (at the marginal level of 0·05), between School 1 and School C.

In the fourth year, for sub-scale 1, none of the project schools obtained significantly lower scores than any other, but Schools B and C (as well as School 12) scored significantly higher than the lowest ranking school, School 8. For sub-scale 2, School D obtained a significantly lower score than eight other schools. For sub-scale 3, School B is again low in the ranking, but differences were not significant except between Schools C and D and between the three highest ranking schools and School 8. For sub-scale 4, School C scored significantly above four schools, including A and D, while School 8 was significantly below all the others. None of the differences for sub-scales 5 and 6 was significant.

The high ranking of School C in the fourth year on sub-scale 3 (self-concept as successful pupil) may well be related to the emphases on collaborative work and social education prevailing in that school. It is interesting to note that in School B, girls score low on self-concept as successful pupil, but high on appreciation of teacher and high on acceptance of school ethos. But it is doubtful if this reflects the influence of the project. On the other hand, the relatively low morale in the leavers' group in School D may well have been exacerbated by the failure of the project in that school to live up to its earlier promise. (It will be recalled that the work with social education was largely taken over by the project workers, and this fact alone would sharpen any existing tensions.)

Comment

In relation to the impact of the project on the schools, the findings from this measure must be taken with extreme caution, since what was measured were attitudes to aspects of the school rather than social education itself. With this reservation, one may risk two tentative conclusions. First, that when the ideas (and ideals) of social education fully imbue the work of the school, as in School C, there will be less tendency to disillusionment among pupils as they reach the end of their school career. The results from School B may partially support this conclusion, although the general ethos of School B was in fact very subject-orientated even in the lowest streams. As against this, one must recall that in School A the project work went furthest in involving the pupils in the community. There is, however, a possible explanation in that not all the pupils were so involved, and the variance in School A, especially for the overall scale, was substantially higher than it was in any other school. One must infer that attitude to school varied more widely here than is usual.

The second tentative conclusion is negative. Attitudes in School D were in general less favourable than in most other schools. This may well be due to the fact that, in the third year of the project when the test was given, the social education work was being done outside the framework of the usual activities of the school. Clearly, for social education to succeed within a school it is essential to win over the majority of relevant staff. In some schools there are bound to be initial difficulties, and these may in fact make for increased problems (for example of discipline) during a transitional period. This point will be returned to in the next chapter.

More generally, it must be stressed that what was measured were the attitudes of selected groups of children in the lower streams of these schools. It would be quite impermissible to make any overall judgements on the relative success of the schools concerned on this slender basis, when even year-to-year differences have not been considered.

On the methodological side, despite the limitations of the standardization, it is suggested that the scale that was developed can prove generally useful in evaluating the work of the secondary school. It will need to be revised in some directions (e.g. there are too few items covering sub-scale 6), and re-standardized over a wider ability range. The authors hope to do this as a separate exercise.

Impact on the community*

The change in the emphases of the project that took place in 1969 entailed concentrating the work in the schools themselves and abandoning the attempt to promote the ends of social education concurrently by working directly with parents and community organizations. It was inevitable, in the light of these changes, that the impact of the work on the surrounding community would be small, particularly in view of the fact that, even in School A, the involvement of groups of pupils in area surveys and community work had been maintained over a period of less than two years at the time of the evaluation. Nevertheless, it was anticipated that the interest of the pupils in the life of the surrounding community and its problems might well have been sufficient to effect some change in attitude within their own homes. At the very least, the pupils' own parents might be expected to be aware of what was being attempted and some might be willing to express their own views about it. At the same time an attempt was made to obtain some idea of the extent to which the activities of the project schools in the field of social education had become public knowledge in that area and of the degree of support that existed for such activities.

Thus this part of the evaluation fell into two parts. The first took the form of interviews with parents, while the second involved interviews with a limited number of unrelated persons chosen to represent certain broad bands within the community as a whole. Sampling in both areas was narrow, however, and the findings should therefore be treated with caution.

Interviews with parents were confined to a sample of sixteen, four from each of the schools. The names and addresses were supplied to the interviewers by the schools, each of which had been asked to offer the names of two children who had seemingly benefited from participation in the project and two who apparently had not.

Interviews were conducted in the evening in the parents' homes, with both interviewers participating, although one or other invariably took the lead, leaving his colleague to act as recorder and prompter. The form of the interview was

* This section was written in collaboration with P. Henry and J. Thomas (Advanced Diploma students from Nottingham University School of Education).

based on a somewhat fuller schedule than that used in interviews with teachers, and coverage was wide. After introducing themselves as educationists interested in the work of the relevant school, the interviewers proceeded to ask parents about the child's attitude to school, his interests, his favourite subjects, his ambitions. Questions were also asked about his activities at home, especially in helping with the chores about the house. Further questions related to friends and clubs. Finally, questions were asked about the child's attitudes, his maturity, the degree of interest he showed in the community and affairs around him.

The actual conduct of the interview varied greatly from one home to another. In some cases few questions were asked since the mother or father spontaneously anticipated most of the questions that might have been asked. In others, the order of questions as well as their form was varied in order to adapt to the flow of the conversation. However, in no case did the interviewer deliberately mention social education until the parent had been given ample opportunity to offer a spontaneous mention in response to questions about school work and the child's attitudes in general. Only if the project was not mentioned spontaneously, were more direct questions asked.

The following are two examples of reports made by the interviewers following the interview:

Mother interviewed. Extreme suspicion at first, rapidly warmed to the subject. Interview in kitchen. Obviously caught in middle of family wash. Kitchen untidy but reasonably clean. Mother obviously bit of a 'rough diamond' but with an advanced concept of community and family. Pamela one of seven children. Mother enthusiastic about the help given by the daughter both to herself and to others in the neighbourhood. Considers that the girl has always shown considerable interest in helping others. Pamela wants to go on to work with handicapped people. Career choice considered by the mother to have always been apparent (no influence from the school). Child has always liked school. Doesn't talk much about school at home. Mother hesitatingly mentioned subject which might be social education. When pressed on the subject confirmed that this was the subject daughter had talked about. (Not given too much weight by the interviewers.) Family as whole obviously brought up to care for each other and for others. (A long anecdote of a brother who on his paper round had made and lit fires for old age pensioners. Equally, mother discussed the problems of having her grandmother living with them for four years and the house was at the time of the interview full with her children and her son's, whose wife was apparently miscarrying.) Mother expressed enthusiasm for the idea of

79

social education in the schools. She considered it would reinforce her own standards which she tried to instil into her family. Both interviewers impressed by what seemed to be a very healthy, socially aware background of family life. However, there was no obvious overt impact of social education upon the family or the child. (School B)

Both parents interviewed. The father dominated the discussion. He displayed aggressive tendencies but was in fact both interested and co-operative. The interview was conducted in the lounge. There were obvious signs of a nouveau riche atmosphere. A large colour television, which became the first subject of discussion, an immaculate but uncomfortable garden and a well-if over-furnished house straight out of *House and Garden*. There was also a new, unused car in the driveway. The father appeared to consider that his image required him to show social awareness, by being a governor of a local comprehensive and youth club. Both interviewers suspected his motives.

He displayed martinet tendencies when momentarily interrupted by his younger child (a boy of ten or eleven). There were two children in the family. He was, however, obviously concerned about the child at school. He knew both the staff and the philosophy of the school. He also referred to the headmaster by his first name – possibly in an attempt to impress. Social education was mentioned in the diatribe and the family had obviously discussed the course and work with the son. The father accepted responsibility for initiating the project work on the 'Probation Service' which the son had done as a contribution to the area profile done by the school. He considered that social education was a necessary part of the school curriculum and his son's development and he expressed the view that social education should be an integral part of any secondary-school curriculum.

Despite the antipathy the father's attitude and the family background aroused in the interviewers it was apparent that social education had aroused interest in the child and this had been communicated to the parents. (School C)

Two further examples are given in Appendix C (pages 159–60). One is unique in that the mother (of a pupil in School A) reports what she takes to be a quite dramatic change as a direct result of work in social education.

While this is the only case of a dramatic change of heart encountered in these interviews, it is apparent from Table 6 that in Schools A and C three of the four interviews allow one to infer that the work of the project had made some impression on the family as well as the pupil, however temporary. The table gives a summary of the sixteen reports, indicating whether or not there was spontaneous

80

Table 6 Summary of reports

School and interviewee	Interview easy	Mother favourable to school	Child favourable to school	Mother spontaneously mentions social education	Child has mentioned social education	Child talks much about social education	Mother favourable to social education	Child favourable to social education	Interviewers conclude social education has altered attitude of family to social questions	Comment
A1*	Yes	Yes	Yes	Yes	Yes	Yes	Yes	Yes	Yes, much	Marked change
2	No	NK	NK	No	Yes	Yes	Yes	Yes	Yes	⎰Much prompting needed
3	Yes	Yes	Yes	No	Yes	NK	Yes	Yes	(Yes)	⎱
4	Yes	NK	NK	No	Yes	NK	Yes	(Yes)	No	
B1†	Yes	NK	Yes	Yes	Yes	No	Yes	Yes	No	⎰Family already community- and help-minded
2	(B) No	(Yes)	NK	No	No	No	D	NK	No	⎰Parents not spontaneous
3	(F) Yes	(No)	No	NK	Yes	No	(Yes)	NK	No	⎰F more keen than child
4	No	(No)	No	No	No	No	(No)	(No)	No	⎰F clearly seeking to impress
C1†	(B) Yes	Yes	NK	Yes	Yes	Yes	Yes	Yes	Yes	
2	(F) No	NK	NK	No	NK	NK	NK	NK	NK	⎰F self-centred, child more in contact with M
3	(Yes)	(Yes)	NK	Yes	Yes	Yes	Yes	Yes	Yes	
4	(B) Yes	NK	Yes	Yes	Yes	Yes	Yes	Yes	(Yes)	⎰Respondents rather inarticulate
D1	(F) Yes	NK	Yes	No	NK	NK	No	NK	No	⎰F a Scot, critical of English education
2*	(B) Yes	Yes	No	No	No	No	D	NK	No	
3	Yes	D	NK	No	No	No	Yes	NK	No	⎰M suspicious and hostile
4	No	No	NK	No	No	No	No	NK	No	

* Interview report reproduced in Appendix C.   † Interview report reproduced in body of text.

In Column 1 F indicates father, B indicates both. Elsewhere the mother (M) is the sole respondent. Qualification of 'Yes' or 'No' is shown by brackets. The letters D and NK denote 'doubtful' and 'not known'.

mention of social education, whether the child talked much about it to the parents, and whether the attitudes of parents and child (as seen by the parent) were favourable.

It is interesting to note that all four parents interviewed in School A expressed support for the ideas of social education and, more significantly, in this school every one of the four children had mentioned the work, while two had talked about it a great deal. These propositions are not equalled in any of the other three schools, although the interviews from School C are nearly as favourable. Taking the table as a whole, it is seen that among the sixteen interviews five parents spontaneously mention social education in response to general questioning about school activities, nine parents indicate that the child has mentioned the work and five report frequent mention; ten parents are clearly favourable, while three are classed as hostile, and in six cases the interviewers concluded that the programme had had some influence on attitudes within the family as a whole, as well as on the attitude of the pupil directly involved.

In addition to the interviews with parents, an attempt was made to obtain some impression of the wider impact of the project by means of random interviews with representatives of certain pre-determined groups within the community area. The groups selected for such sampling were: (a) youth leaders, (b) librarians, (c) local shopkeepers, (d) old age pensioners. In the case of School C, the investigators also spoke to the receptionist at the local sports centre, and for School D one bus conductor was seen.

The form of questioning was more varied than it was for the interviews with parents, but whenever applicable the following points were raised:

> Could the interviewee identify the pupils of the school concerned? Did he ever experience any trouble with them? More or less than with pupils of other schools? Were they more or less responsible than they had been in the past? Did they help within the area where help was needed? Did they talk about problems in the area? The interviewee was also told that some of the pupils were receiving lessons 'to make them more socially aware', and asked what he thought of the idea.

These interviews, conducted at random in shops and libraries, etc., and sometimes in the street, involved a total of nine respondents in Area B, ten in Area C and eleven in each of Areas A and D. The results are summarized below.

Area A

The owner of the post office revealed that she was aware of social education. She thought it a good thing. She did not, however, have much contact with children

82

from the subject school, but had a son who attended it. She felt that the children were becoming more aware of their communities and more independent and mature in their relationships. She was, however, critical of the books children were encouraged to read and objected strongly to

> essay questions which divide the family and questionnaires which pry into private family matters.

The owner of a corner shop in the vicinity of the school said that she had been in the area for seven years. She found the children pleasant and helpful and revealed that she was aware of social education and the community work being done by senior children from the school. This local awareness of social education was further confirmed by the owner of a local grocery store. She stated that she knew of community work being undertaken by children from the school. She expressed her approval of the project, commenting:

> It makes children aware of their community and is a good preparation for later life.

The awareness of the general public of the work in social education in the school was further confirmed by brief interviews conducted in the street. The four pensioners interviewed all showed knowledge of community research and work by the school. The local librarian was unable to supply any relevant information. Nor was the leader of one youth club. Indeed, the latter firmly thrust responsibility for the 'disgraceful behaviour' of his members on the lack of discipline in schools. The leader of another youth club was more positive, however. He felt that there had been a general increase and improvement in social awareness on the part of his members over the last two or three years. He claimed a membership of some 1900 drawn from all over Nottingham. He felt that he would be unable to identify School A from these. But he claimed that his club was engaged in extensive social work in the neighbourhood and felt that, as these children were from the immediate area, they were probably playing a major role.

Area B

Both youth leaders interviewed in this area felt there had been a deterioration in the behaviour of girls over the past three years. However, the leader of the youth club suspected that he had no girls who were directly concerned with the social education project. Librarians were unable to make any significant or relevant comments. There were few local shops where it was probable that girls

83

from the subject school could be identified as such. However, the manager of a local branch of one chain store had a vague idea of the kind of work in social education being attempted in the school and commented that:

> The [School B] girls seem to have more purpose about them and they seem to be much more individually responsible than girls from other schools I am familiar with.

The manageress of a neighbouring shop had no significant observations to make. Nor did any of the old age pensioners spoken to, although one of these did comment that he thought that the girls' behaviour had shown marked improvement lately.

Area C

The receptionist of the sports centre used both casually and officially by the school could not identify any significant difference in behaviour. However, she was at pains to point out that the children were certainly not members of the trouble-making minority. The owner of the grocery/confectionery shop said the children used her shop continuously. She had only been in the shop since the previous November and the former owners had discouraged children from using the premises. She found the children polite and well-behaved, and there had been no pilfering or trouble of any kind from the children. The manageress of the post office close to the school was generally critical of the behaviour of local schoolchildren. Under pressure she identified local grammar-school children as being particularly bothersome in comparison with the project school. She had not heard of social education.

The manager of the supermarket adjoining the post office, on the other hand, had heard of social education. His premises were used in social education projects (for the pricing of groceries, etc.). He approved of the scheme and indicated his willingness to continue to be used as a source of material.

The local librarian was unable to provide evidence of any significantly different behaviour. But the conductor and driver of a bus agreed that there was a significant difference between the behaviour of project children and the pupils from other secondary schools in the area. The old age pensioners living locally had all received visits from the children, but most appeared to have relatives near at hand and had not therefore pursued the tendered offer of help. They were nevertheless appreciative of the offer and of the maturity and responsibility of the children.

84

The local youth leader described the subject school's children as easily the

> . . . most active, responsible and socially aware . . .

of the children who were members of his club.

> They know what they want to do and participate fully in all of our club activities. They even on occasion initiate their own!

However, he was not merely aware of social education but had been actively involved in group leadership and project work by the staff. This had included the use of the club facilities for discussions and group activities.

AREA D

The manager of the supermarket opposite the school confirmed that the children used his shop both for making purchases and for topic and project work and investigations. He found the older children (i.e. those working on social education) to be well-behaved and responsible. What little trouble he had was from the younger pupils.

The owner of the local post office (in the central area of the village) compared the behaviour of the project school children in a favourable light with that of local grammar-school pupils.

One old age pensioner interviewed in the street had heard at second hand that children were helping pensioners with their shopping, housework, etc. She, and other pensioners interviewed, found the children from the project school pleasant and responsible.

The interviews with three librarians revealed nothing significant regarding the behaviour or book-borrowing habits of the children.

The interview with the youth leader also revealed no evidence of a significant change in behaviour.

Comment

In view of the relatively short period during which the project was in operation, and especially the rather limited involvement with the community that it engendered, the above results are highly encouraging. It is clear that social education has generally made sufficient impact on the pupils to cause them to talk about the work at home. Often, it was the only subject mentioned. In three of the areas, at least some of the random interviews revealed awareness and approval of the work.

Finally, despite the limitations of sampling, it is clear that the impact of the work on the community was most apparent in Area A, where this aspect received the greatest attention, and in Area C, where the work of the school as a whole was animated by objectives similar to those which had inspired the project itself.

Additional procedures

As noted in the introduction to this chapter, at least two additional procedures were used in the attempt to assess the effectiveness of the project. Both entailed comparisons between the four project schools and the eight control schools mentioned earlier. The first was defined as a measure of the degree of self-understanding shown by these students as well as their ability to assess their fellows correctly. The second was an attempt to assess their relative ability to participate actively and constructively in group discussion. The reason for focusing on these two kinds of skill is at once apparent, since these are among the basic social skills which an effective programme of social education might be expected to promote. In the event, neither measure proved to be a reliable discriminator, and our account will, therefore, be brief.

A single procedure was adopted to measure self-understanding and assessment of peers. Fourth-year groups in the project schools and comparable groups in the control schools were randomly assigned to small sub-groups, each consisting of 4 to 6 members. Within these smaller sub-groups, every member was given the task of rating himself and every other member of the group on two dimensions: outgoing or reserved, and stable or worried. These were chosen as the two most basic dimensions of variation in human personality as they emerge from the numerous studies of Burt, Eysenck, Cattell and many others.* They may conveniently be referred to as extraversion and neuroticism, using the terminology of Eysenck. The two dimensions were carefully explained to the students with appropriate illustrations, and their task was simply to locate each individual concerned by placing a cross at one of the intersections on a two-dimensional seven-point grid, separate forms being used for each rater and each ratee.

Scoring was based on the assumption that to the extent that an individual's self-assessments and his peer-assessments were accurate, they would agree with the assessments of his fellows. Accordingly the measure of self-assessment was taken as the mean deviation of the values given to himself by each rater (for each dimension), from the ratings made of him by each of the other raters (3–5 in all). Similarly, the estimate of peer-assessment was the mean deviation of the ratings

* See, for example, F. W. Warburton, 'The assessment of personality traits', in *Development in Learning*, Vol. III: Contexts of Education, ed. J. F. Morris and E. A. Lunzer (Staples, 1969); H. J. Eysenck, *Dimensions of Personality* (Routledge & Kegan Paul, 1950); and R. B. Cattell, *The Scientific Analysis of Personality* (Penguin Books, 1965).

of any given rater from those of each other independent rater, taking each of them in turn. For each of these calculations, self-ratings by the rater were excluded. Thus, in a group of four raters, the score for each was a mean of 3 means, each of these in turn being a mean of 2 means (omitting self-ratings for each comparison in turn). Separate scores were obtained for extraversion and neuroticism.

Calculation of these scores, which might otherwise have been tedious, was carried out by the computer using a specially devised program. Differences between groups within schools and differences between schools (based on means for their constituent groups) were examined in separate analyses of variance. The results showed that, in nearly all schools, there was significant variation between the randomly chosen sub-groups. This finding alone seriously weakens the force of the comparisons between schools. Significant differences were also found here, however, and Table 7 shows the rank order of school means for

Table 7   Rank order of schools for agreement with peers in self-ratings and in peer-ratings (near to distant)

Self-ratings: extraversion	8	3(B)	6	4	1	2	5	9(C)	10(A)	11	12	7(D)
Self-ratings: neuroticism	8	6	9(C)	2	1	12	4	3(B)	10(A)	11	5	7(D)
Peer-ratings: extraversion	11	3(B)	7(D)	6	4	10(A)	2	5	1	9(C)	12	8
Peer-ratings: neuroticism	11	4	6	3(B)	10(A)	2	12	9(C)	9	7(D)	1	8

each of the four variables, i.e. (1) agreement of self-ratings with ratings received from peers (extraversion), (2) the same measure (neuroticism), (3) agreement of groups in rating one another, excluding all self-ratings (extraversion), and (4) the same measure (neuroticism).

Any attempt to account for the differences shown in Table 7 would clearly be speculative. The four project schools do not cluster at either extreme, nor is it possible to account for the order of the project schools themselves on the basis of known variations in the success of the social education programme. It would be rash to reject the hypothesis that the differences obtained are due to errors of sampling combined with uncontrolled factors in the relevant school populations. Nor would one place much importance on these results in view of the significance of variations among sub-groups within schools.

The following comments should be made as a pointer to future studies. The present technique was devised in preference to a combination of sentence completion and 'guess who' techniques,* partly out of interest in its potential, and partly to avoid making undue demands on the control schools – since in the absence of opportunities for discussion and implementation, such techniques as 'guess who' might quite rightly be rejected as actually being damaging to morale. The technique adopted proved readily acceptable both to pupils and to schools, as well as economical in time. It might yield less ambiguous results in future studies if attention is given to certain defects:

1 It was a mistake to restrict the size of sub-groups to 4–6. Sub-groups of 10–12 would have been manageable for the pupils, and the results would have been more stable.

2 The use of peer-agreement as the sole measure of accuracy of estimate cannot be accepted without some empirical validation. Ratings by teachers, or by psychologists, might well have been used as controls. The technique should also be validated by reference to objective questionnaires and/or performance measures. In the present state of our ignorance, it is interesting to speculate that agreement among peers might just as well be taken as an index of stereotypy – with disagreement showing independence of judgement – which would lead to a complete reversal of the predictions that were made in regard to the effects of social education.

An interesting finding was that, in general, the students' self-rating on extraversion came closer to the ratings assigned to them by peers than did their self-ratings on neuroticism. By contrast, inter-peer agreement (excluding self-ratings) was greater for neuroticism than it was for extraversion.

The last technique was designed to assess effectiveness in contributing to a constructive discussion. Since it proved even less successful, the account can be brief. Once again, the same procedure was used with fourth-year pupils in project and control schools. Within each school, the group was divided into up to six discussion groups, each containing 6–15 individuals. They were shown a film depicting a family quarrel (the Czech film *Peter and Pavla* which features a strained situation between father and adolescent son, but also involves other characters, mother and friend, whose roles are ambiguous) to provide a stimulus for discussion. The resulting discussion was helped when necessary by prompts from the group-leader (once again diploma students served in this capacity). Transcripts of the ensuing discussions were then analysed for effectiveness of contributions. It was decided to categorize each contribution, using six categories. The first three were to be used to record constructiveness of relevant

* See R. B. Cunningham, *Understanding Group Behaviour of Boys and Girls* (Teachers' College, Columbia University, 1951).

contributions. Thus the lowest score would be used for remarks which were relevant, but non-constructive, being no more than reflections by the contributor about his own personal experience, triggered off by the discussion. The second category was used for relevant and constructive contributions. The third was used for contributions that were not merely relevant but also showed insight. The remaining three categories were used for various kinds of irrelevant interjections and comments. Before examining differences between groups, it was decided to validate the categorization by requiring each of four judges to go through the transcripts, making an independent categorization of each remark. In the event, it was found that inter-judge agreement was too low to warrant proceeding any further with the analysis.

Summary and conclusion

It was stressed at the beginning of this chapter that the aim of an evaluation study in the context of a project of this kind is necessarily a limited one. It is not to establish whether the programme that was implemented is the best that could be devised, nor even whether it has been shown to secure overall results that are superior to those achieved in other settings. There are too many ways for schools to differ to enable one to achieve adequate controls for valid comparisons to be made. Moreover, the aims of schools tend to differ in important ways, so that even if it were shown that 'treated' schools were more successful in achieving one set of aims, it might well be the case that the others were successful in achieving a different set of aims. To this one must add that there are no objective methods of evaluating one set of aims against another.

The object of the present evaluation was the limited one of establishing whether and how far the project proved acceptable to teachers and to pupils, whether its objectives were appreciated and seen to be relevant, and whether, and to what extent, they had been reached. Given these restricted aims, our conclusions may be stated quite briefly. (More detailed summaries are given after each of the more important sections.)

1   It is clear that in three of the four schools the teachers most closely involved in the project had been largely won over to its aims. Moreover, despite certain reservations which a number of them retained about its implementation, the majority believed it to have proved the viability of a programme of social education, even for the academically less able. Above all, they were agreed about the advantages of giving pupils a greater share of responsibility.

2   The pupils in all four schools were almost unanimous in their approval of

the programme as they had experienced it. In at least two of the schools, they expressed an appreciable understanding of its true objectives.

3   In at least two of the schools, it was found that attitude to school as a whole had apparently not fallen off in the fourth year but was actually more favourable than that shown in the third year of schooling.

4   In at least two of the schools, it could be shown that several people in the community were aware of what was being tried and approved of it. Also, the majority of parents in those schools gave their support to the work.

5   In one of the four schools, the project appeared to have failed in many of its aims. The reasons would seem to be lack of continuity in the work, errors made in the initial stages and perhaps a certain clash of aims between the school and the project team.

V. Social education in action

Our experience in trying to explain what we have been doing to varied groups of people – teachers, wives, friends, children, professors of education and students – is that the best method of making things clear is to describe actual incidents as they occurred in schools. These incidents, and our comments on them, illustrate our view of what social education is all about. They give a flavour of what social education means 'at the coal face'. They permit listeners and readers to interpret the incidents for themselves. Often their interpretation will be quite different from ours. This chapter has deliberately been written in such a way as to enable readers to form their own judgements on the basis of the material presented. Some may find themselves perceiving things which we ourselves have overlooked.

1. Pupil responsibility

Our assumption has been that children are capable of taking decisions for themselves and planning concerted action. It follows that the teacher must create situations in which decisions can be taken by children. We attempted this with one fourth-year group in the following way.

Our work for the term was to be based on an examination of the groups to which the class members belonged, with particular emphasis on peer groups. In order to establish from the beginning the importance (to them) of group membership, we decided to begin with one of us attacking them as a class and picking arbitrarily upon two individuals.

The following is an extract from Wyn Williams's diary, and describes a series of events that took place in School D during the third year of the project:

> Accordingly, I went into the class and rapidly forced them to fold their arms, sit up straight, watch me and then take down a number of rules of conduct which I expected them to observe. They reacted quickly, if sullenly, to all these instructions, and I then excused myself and left. John took over and remarked that my conduct had rather embarrassed him and perhaps he could attempt to speak to me privately about it if they wished. They complained bitterly about being treated like 12-year-olds (which suggests something about their expectations, and perhaps about their experience,

of the way in which 12-year-olds are treated) and about the unfairness of attacks upon individuals in the class. One boy then suggested I be called back so that they could tell me of their complaints. This was done. The change in my manner now led them to realize that we had deliberately staged the attack to show how they resented attacks on individual group members and the way they had been collectively spoken to, and to show them that the problem was how to persuade such a teacher to change. The lesson led us to suggest that perhaps we ought to treat them not as 12-year-olds but as 18-year-olds – adding three years to their age rather than subtracting three. A discussion followed as to what changes of behaviour would be required both from us and from them.

Following this discussion, it was agreed that the group itself should assume more responsibility for control of behaviour within the classroom. It would also be more involved in planning future activities. A class committee of five was appointed by the group to act as an executive for regulating behaviour, and to be the spokesmen for the group as a whole.

This example of an attempt to put into practice the assumption that children can organize and take decisions and make choices has important implications. One is that once a decision has been accepted, it is important to ensure that it is carried through.

In this case we found plenty of interest over the next five weeks, but little indication that the class really were going to control their activities and plan them. Things came to a head with the failure of a large number to do some work between one week and the next. (This class, being composed of leavers, was not set homework like other classes in the school.)

Accordingly, we decided that it was essential to present the class with a choice. They could decide whether homework should or should not be done and they should decide whether they wanted the social education lessons to continue or not. We stated that:

a the decisions were theirs and the session ought, therefore, to be conducted by the class committee in our absence;
b our rights, as concerned adults, included the right to refuse to accept a simple 'We want you to continue'. A case had to be made by them, and they would need to show that it was a convincing one.

The class was very uncertain as to their ability to handle the situation. One girl remarked that the boys would shout the girls down, and another predicted chaos. However, the majority wanted to try and we withdrew. Twenty minutes later, the committee called us. The class was angry and frustrated. Chaos had ensued, they said. We must return to help them run the class. We refused. They were perfectly capable of running the session and taking the two decisions, we said. We would discuss committee procedure with them for two minutes and then leave them to it. Once more we withdrew. We were recalled to hear their decisions five minutes before the end of the double period.

They did not wish to do homework, arguing that their home and job commitments were too great. However, a solution would be for five minutes to be knocked off each lesson during the day. This would result in a total period of half an hour which would then be used to complete unfinished work or for doing homework.

Secondly, social education should continue because (a) they found it interesting and relevant, and (b) they had come to recognize that they could run things for themselves without our help and would like to do so again. As one boy remarked, 'When you said you were going to treat us as 18-year-olds, we didn't believe you. Then after a few weeks we realized you were serious, but we thought it was silly, because we are only 15. But today, we really did it, didn't we? We *were* like 18-year-olds, and it was great!'

Before drawing conclusions from this illustration, it may be profitable to consider the outcome of giving responsibility to children in other project schools.

In all project schools this decision meant (a) giving children the task of doing their part of the class's survey work in the area in groups of two or three without teacher supervision – this involved interviewing adults who might be in an official position (e.g. a health visitor, a councillor), or members of the general public, such as old age pensioners; (b) giving children the responsibility of framing their interview schedules and collating and presenting the information obtained; (c) giving them the responsibility of deciding what action, if any, ought to be taken when surveys were complete.

The problems that arose were many. The first was the problem of the difficult interview. It is a situation which even adults may find hard to handle. The following are two illustrations based on the diary records kept by the teacher who collaborated on the project.

In School B, the incident involved pupils from 3C who went to the health centre with questions prepared for the dental health officer and found themselves facing the eye specialist. They panicked and continued to ask the questions which they had prepared for the dental officer, thereby greatly annoying the eye specialist, who complained to the school. Clearly there is always a danger

93

that busy adults may be unsympathetic towards a group of unsure adolescents.

During the course of work on a school profile, in School C, children in the third year interviewed the head, deputy head and senior staff about their functions in the school. The teacher was not present during this interviewing and a number of teachers took exception to the questions that were put. The teacher commented that he himself would have found it hard to handle such an interview situation.

Another problem arising from giving this kind of responsibility is that children can avoid doing what they have been allowed out of school to do. The temptation to evade work exists, and occasionally the work will not be done at all. In practice, however, such occasions were very rare (see Chapter IV).

The third problem derives from the difficulty of avoiding blunders. When they are unsupervised, children can and do make mistakes. A group of four girls in School B, having participated in an area survey, decided that one old lady in particular needed help. In the event, they took such an active interest in her that she came to feel threatened by the situation. While visiting her, one of the four took the opportunity to smoke and swear – as she found natural when at home. This upset the old lady. The final straw came when one of the group asked for a drink of water and was offered milk. She poured it away because it was sour. The old lady's feelings were hurt and she complained to the school.

The last incident clearly illustrates a source of difficulty which is unavoidable. But one might add that, while problems cannot always be avoided, it is usually possible to profit by mistakes. And sometimes mistakes can be put right. Had the episode been acted out with the class, had it been discussed with a view to finding out what went wrong and how it could have been avoided, the blunder itself would have presented a real chance for the class to recognize for themselves differences between adult expectations about manners and their own. The girls clearly lacked the social awareness and the skills to get on with the old lady. Perhaps, too, this incident might have been avoided altogether. It illustrates dramatically the need for thorough preparation of children through discussion, practice interviewing and socio-drama before engaging in the real thing.

As already noted in Chapter IV, the teachers in the project school who taught social education were largely in favour of taking the risks involved in giving responsibility, on the grounds that the benefits outweighed the risks.

In the first place, children who have made a mistake through a lack of social awareness and social skill, in a situation where they have decided to take action and have failed, are much more anxious to rectify the mistake than children who are constantly exhorted to show good manners to adults but can see no clear reason why they should. In the second place, delegation of responsibility gives

94

children the chance to develop the social skills necessary to elicit co-operation rather than hostility from adults. Finally, the children themselves recognize that when teachers allow them to go out of school collecting information, and when they allow them to determine what should be done about that information, the teachers are showing a trust in their sense of responsibility. The awareness is seldom lost.

2. The role of the teacher

If the assumption is made that to be responsible for their own behaviour and to decide what they wish to do are good choices for children to make, then there is a responsibility on the part of the teacher to accept the consequences of the assumption, and to create situations in which the implications of what the children and teacher have jointly decided can be worked out. Consistency is not to be expected in the initial stages from teachers or children in such situations, and we found that the success of any one particular session did not mean that our troubles, or theirs, were over. For instance, in the last session an attempt to get pupils involved in planning the next term's activities led us to express our disgust at the low level of response and led the class to request our withdrawal while they ran a session to come up with suggestions.

Not only lack of consistency, but the knowledge that some children and colleagues will see this type of situation as abdication of responsibility at best, or a waste of time at worst, will nearly always make teachers realize that this way of working with children is far from easy or free from stress. In our view it is important to make clear to children and teachers that to allow the former to take responsibility for their own activities is less restful, but also far more stimulating, than a system in which the teacher is solely responsible for organizing and decision-making.

One interview in the evaluation (carried out in July 1970) involved a teacher in School A. She commented,

> When I first came in September, I found 2B a very, very difficult form in many ways. They resented practically everything you tried to do, and I obviously started on the wrong foot with them. But when the Social Education Project was handed over to me, I gave them a fortnight in which they could have a free hand to do a class profile and tackle it the way they wanted. During that fortnight I had a chance, many chances, to talk to children individually and make suggestions, and they gained confidence from the fact that they were left to do it on their own. This followed my

95

change of attitude as well, I think, because it did need a change of attitude. I was *not* directing so much, any longer, as leading, and by the end of the fortnight they were beginning to look forward to their lessons and they were far more sensitive in their approach to me in particular.

This is a good example of how a teacher can change her role from information-giver and disciplinarian to senior colleague working with junior colleagues. We believe that this change, while difficult to achieve permanently, can come quite quickly, as in the illustration above. The implications are far-reaching. The teacher who seeks to carry out social education has to create an 'open classroom'.* That is, a place where:

a the teacher yields up *some* power to pupils so that they can make genuine choices;

b the teacher is an adult with a personality of his own that others have to recognize, i.e. it is not a permissive classroom if by this is meant a room where children do exactly as they please—if the teacher is annoyed at someone's behaviour he ought to express it;

c most decisions affecting the running of the class are *communal* decisions;

d the development of workable alternative strategies to authoritarian control has to take place.

Let us be quite clear that in our view the authoritarian teacher is not necessarily an uninteresting or bad teacher. Indeed, a teacher who is authoritarian and carefully plans his work often is caring and efficient, and children like him because they know he cares for them and they know what is expected of them. However, this is very different from the open classroom approach. The difference is perhaps best illustrated by an extract from the diary of a teacher in School A:

> This may be its most important contribution. Within the context of social education I am not omniscient; I am struggling to understand and am only slightly less puzzled than [the boy] is; in some areas he is less puzzled than I am. Not knowing the answers, I cannot be dogmatic about them. Hence I am open to question; that is, I am no longer a teacher, but simply another human being. Dialogue is possible.

Here the teacher's role is central. A man who was tremendously interested in his individual relationships with children commented in his interview that he gave children the opportunity to work on projects of their own within his mathematics

* H. R. Kohl, *The Open Classroom: a Practical Guide to a New Way of Teaching* (Methuen, 1970).

lesson. The only difference made by the social education work was that it provided a context in which he could talk to children with the 'guards down'.

3. Surveys: preparation, execution and follow-up

Allowing children to carry out surveys as a result of decisions which they had helped to make brought further problems, and created further opportunities. If it is true that social education is a process during which children acquire more advanced skills, it follows that survey work in an area ought not to take place until the basic skills of observation and communication have been thoroughly learned. Thus the profiles of the class and the school, or some aspect of them, need to precede any examination of the area around the school. Through work on these profiles, the children gain an opportunity to decide what they are going to look for when they set out to do an area profile; they can practise interviewing techniques with people they know, and they have a chance in socio-drama to simulate situations with which they may come face to face outside school. For example, the teacher can play the part of an awkward adult.

The experience in project schools indicates that it is not the age of the children but their experience of the required skills that is decisive. Teachers in two schools remarked that second- and third-year pupils working on very specific, limited surveys outside school were perfectly capable of coping after training, whereas untrained fourth years were not. In School D, an attempt to do a large-scale survey of an area (1200 households in all) proved a failure because those involved (a) were not clear what problems they were trying to investigate, (b) had no experience in interviewing, and (c) had no skills in handling and presenting the information when it was gathered. Surveys should be exercises in awareness and not statistical overviews. Indeed, few teachers have the skills required for conducting valid statistical compilations.

In another project school (School A), the teacher remarked that the fourth year 'have been given too much responsibility too late – they just did not know what to do with so much freedom'.

In addition, the time allotted, though plentiful (210 minutes a week), was wrongly allocated:

Mondays	2.55–4.05 p.m.	70
Tuesdays	1.30–2.40 p.m.	70
Fridays	2.55–4.05 p.m.	70
		210 minutes

Two afternoons would have been better from an organizational point of view, particularly when rooms did not adjoin and suitable exhibition and work space was not available.

There was also inadequate planning and discussion, and this resulted in confusion over the aims and methods to be used. The 'team' was not a team. Some staff involved welcomed the opportunity of allowing children a say in planning and organization, others resented it and wanted a formally structured programme. Finally, the decision to involve two fourth-year groups (4B and 4C) led to resentment on their part. The classes quite deliberately tried to retain their separate identity.

The emphasis on getting children in social education to build their own surveys, and carry them out, leads to a number of situations that need careful consideration by anyone embarking on such work.

One of the dangers of over-ambitious large-scale surveys of an area is that of annoying large numbers of people: 'Not more bloody kids asking questions.' The survey that can only be done once is of little value. Thus the survey of the whole village of 1200 households, as was recognized by the teachers involved, could hardly have been repeated even if it had been desirable. The answer to this problem is to do a social topography of the area first (see Appendix B), and then to take a limited problem for investigation. Thus, finding out the facilities available for play for the under-fives in an area can be a perfectly reasonable project which does not need to be repeated for another few years, and which does not involve interviewing people who are likely to be bothered again by another group of interviewers.

Surveys in the context of social education are *action* surveys, and it is assumed that children will decide when they want some sort of action to follow from a survey. The following illustrations indicate just how much pressure can be felt by the teacher if action is desired by the class.

In the first case, a girl was engaged on a project on play areas and waste areas and how they were used. She surveyed the estate, identifying the waste areas. She then went and asked local people, including a local councillor, all about it. She and her group had proposals for action, but nothing came of them. The teacher commented, 'If I had had the time and resources, I would have followed this up and pushed it a bit.'

In the second case, the teacher comments that area profiles are undertaken with a view to the possibility of being involved in community action but that 'It [action] gets left out because it is the difficult part – and then as a teacher you usually go for things which are easier and leave the difficult bits.'

Both teachers, who were extremely involved with their work, felt the strain of

98

trying to extend their activities into new fields. This feeling is exacerbated when the action is instigated by the youngsters themselves. For the teacher, the sense of lack of control over what happens can be an unnerving experience.

Indeed, an interesting comparison can be made here with community service work, which was also a regular feature of the curriculum in all the project schools. One teacher, commenting on the impact of social education work on the local community, remarked that 'probably more has been done through the RI people with their help with serving meals for old folk in the community centre and helping to clean up yards and gardens . . . this has been an asset to the community and I think something good has come out of it. But this kind of survey that we have done in social education has not done a large amount [for the community].'

This comment highlights two important issues for teachers. The community service work can be carefully controlled – it is teacher-devised and organized and, of course, some children get deeply involved in it.

Secondly, the community service approach guarantees that some kind of activity is undertaken. In social education, the kind of action proposed by the children tends to be less conventional. In an examination of the problem of communicating with local people about the impact on them of the new redevelopment scheme, one boy drew a cartoon which certainly had impact. It depicted bulldozers entering a house while the inhabitants ignored what was happening to them. He wanted to make it into a poster to display locally, showing people the need for them to become more directly involved. The expected reaction of authority to such a display (particularly when they had been making efforts to explain and involve local people in the redevelopment scheme) worried both the teachers and the project staff.

The action proposed was indeed too extreme to contemplate with equanimity. Some hesitation from teachers when certain action is proposed by children can be justifiable. It is true that the action survey may not lead to any action at all. Children may well feel that either there is nothing that needs to be done, or that there is nothing that they want to do or can do about the situation. This cannot be predicted in advance and the teacher has to be content with the knowledge that the skills of interviewing, formulating questions and presenting results involved in doing the survey have made the whole exercise worth while. It must be said, however, that this did not happen in any of the project schools. It is far more likely, as we found, that the surveys will be almost over-productive, in that children will come up with so many ideas that not all of them can be attempted. Indeed, some proposals for action may well be the same as those proposed by the teacher in a community service programme. The big difference is that children become much more involved when the decision has been theirs. They will also have had the experience of discovering needs for themselves, and are consequently more likely to continue to recognize needs when they have left school.

An interesting example of the kind of involvement which occurred is that of the teacher from School A who decided that one situation of fairly immediate relevance to his class was what would happen to them as a result of the redevelopment scheme scheduled for the area. Accordingly, he began by putting on the blackboard the present population figures and those for the future after redevelopment had taken place. The current 14 500 population was to become 5750 over a five-year period. The class's response was immediate – Where would people move? Who decided who should move? How much would the new houses cost? What if people did not want to move? The teacher disclaimed knowledge of any answers to these questions, but suggested that it would be possible for them to find out for themselves if groups were formed in the class to examine different questions. Eleven groups were formed and they spent two terms (two periods a week) working on the study. However, their interviews and costing work led to suggestions about what ought to be done.

One boy proposed a campaign to awaken adult interest in the area in what was going to happen to them. When it was pointed out that the city planning department was trying hard to do just that, and that they had arranged an exhibition, held public meetings and asked for comments on the plans from interested groups, he remarked that his group's interviews had shown that the authority had failed. The class set out to mount an exhibition which would be displayed in launderettes, shops, pubs and doctors' waiting-rooms. This would be more likely to reach people than the planners' exhibition in a large hall. Moreover, the newsletter *Span*, which the school produced jointly with the local grammar school, would appeal to more people in the area if an issue were devoted to contributions from them than city planning department documents. Finally, a poster campaign in the area on 'This is Happening to You' lines might make adults more aware and less fatalistic about what could be achieved. They also interviewed a local councillor who promised to investigate an allegation of victimization made by one old lady against someone in authority. Although not all of these suggestions reached fruition, the children did make a number of suggestions to the local authority, and the great depth of their involvement could not be doubted.

100

4. Effect on the individual

What is a socially educated child like at the end of a process of social education? There can be no ideal model. One can, however, try to illustrate the aims of social education from particular incidents in school. Such a method is more specific and allows for alternative interpretations to our own of how the socially educated person or group should have behaved or did behave.

The following illustration brings out clearly the difficulty of making judgements in this field. On one occasion, a group of girls in School C were asked to take part in a school profile. The teacher's diary shows what happened:

> Initially, every group was asked to define its area and write out an approach. It was at this point that criticisms of the study were first voiced, and this culminated in a class discussion with chairs grouped round my desk. The dissenters (they numbered six girls and four boys) were critical of:
>
> 1. the relevance of interviewing staff;
> 2. the ultimate aim of producing a school booklet (for parents of new-comers to school);
> 3. the usefulness of the facts to be recorded;
> 4. the need to examine in detail the school and its pupils.
>
> The girls especially were extremely sensible during the discussions but did not seem convinced of the validity or relevance of the profile. They argued that you learned to get on with people as you grew older and that there was no need for it to be planned as lessons. They also said that they felt it was more important to study more academic subjects which would be useful when they left school.

This fascinating diary extract reveals that these girls were challenging the basic assumption that explicit examination of relationships helps. They were asserting their right not to take part in something with which they disagreed on coherent grounds. It is difficult to see them as other than mature and responsible. Interestingly, the diary records that later three of the girls did decide to take part and went to assist the local junior school. They were stimulated

a   to write a letter of thanks;
b   to suggest a detailed follow-up;
c   to write a detailed account from the points of view of the head, the pupils and the teachers.

We are interpreting their rejection here as an example of reasonable, mature people turning down a project approach. Their maturity was not the result of

101

doing social education; it was not a behavioural outcome (since the incident occurred in 1969). Our only claim would be that the project was operating in a manner which encouraged the development of this type of response – and quite clearly we are not arguing that this approach is exclusive to social education. The final examples in this chapter are taken from two individuals who were stated to have specifically altered their behaviour in class and at home as a result of doing social education work. This is a large claim, but it is maintained by the boys themselves, their teacher and their parents.

Boy A was the school 'hard man' – a lively, argumentative lad with a great deal of energy and lively intelligence which was not reflected in school work. His relationship with his teacher was excellent because the latter treated him in an adult manner and expected him to plan and execute work for himself (with the group). During a conversation one day on the topic of vandalism, the boy remarked that he had stopped 'doing' telephone boxes. When asked why, he replied that it was the result of doing social education. The teacher expressed disbelief and was told that there were two reasons why this statement was true. In the first place, the interviews with elderly people in the new flats had led to a realization by the group of boys involved of the dependence of old people on the telephone box in emergencies and they had thought for the first time about the consequences of 'doing' a box. Secondly, and very simply, the lad no longer felt bored at school and, in his view, boredom led to a lot of vandalism.

He was a remarkable boy who responded when given a challenge and the responsibility for organizing things himself. The relationship of social education work to his development is highly complex. Certainly, there is the possibility that a whole variety of factors not mentioned here influenced his behaviour, but what the project work did do for him was

a spark off an interest in what was to happen to the new area as a result of redevelopment, and
b encourage him to take responsibility.

It is not suggested that this response could only have been triggered off by social education. What can be said is that in this particular school situation, it was work in social education that provided the opportunities for his development – and that the approach, and the role of teacher as colleague demanded by social education, were decisive. The teacher certainly felt this to be so.

Boy B is a sharply contrasting case. He was a quiet boy at the beginning of the fourth year who was not likely to bring himself to the notice of the teacher. Apparently shy, he was someone who put up with school rather than enjoyed it.

His transformation was due in his mother's view to the impact of his form teacher and the project. He talked of social education work at home and carried out some excellent interviews with a pressure group formed to serve the needs of a similar redevelopment area. His increased confidence in himself led to an interesting situation when he was interviewed for a job with a large motor-car company. He had failed his mathematics test (set by the firm) and in his interview explained that this was partly because he was far more interested in the social education work in which he had been engaged. The personnel manager drew him out on this and they spoke together for forty-five minutes, at the end of which he was given the job. The personnel manager was sufficiently impressed to invite his mother to visit the firm, and asked her about the work he had been doing in school.

The mother wrote to the teacher thanking him for his interest in the boy and commenting upon his involvement in the social education work and the change of attitude which she had noticed in the boy.

These two examples, in our view, indicate that the development of individuals in terms of their social maturity and ability to cope with situations can be achieved as a result of the approach and the content of social education. Other curriculum approaches which stress (a) the teacher's role as fellow explorer, and (b) situations to be examined in which pupils can determine the area of concern and the method of tackling them, might also produce similar types of behaviour.

There is an implication that children will make comparisons between the open classroom situation and others. In School A the new head of humanities re-marked on one occasion that children doing social education had developed an image of what a teacher should be and were inclined to be critical if he did not measure up to it. In his case, he found that the compensatory factor was that those involved in social education responded better when he required the fourth year to do integrated work on a project on 'Leisure', particularly with regard to working in groups and planning their own activities.

There is also an implication that the role change on the part of the teacher will on occasions create, in Kohl's words, 'fear, depression and panic' in teacher and pupil alike, because it rests upon a significant shift in power in the classroom – power which any teacher fears losing (partly from fear of what colleagues will say) and which pupils may be uncertain that they can handle. It was interesting to see how often the few children who did not like social education stated that this was because certain groups took advantage of the freedom and did little work.

Of course children within their own groups also indicate what norms of behaviour are acceptable and sometimes resent close examination of them. In two of the project schools, groups of children queried why they should examine issues that divided them. In one case, the investigation of peer groups led to a

103

renewal of a conflict that they admitted had emerged the year before between 'skinheads' and 'mods'. 'Why do you divide us by asking us to discuss these things?', they asked. They had uncovered a value judgement we make – that it is better to bring issues out into the daylight and try and come to terms with them, rather than to pretend that they do not exist, or bury them. Indeed, this class answered its own question, 'Why study things that upset and divide us?' by saying, in discussion:

a   that understanding people or groups does not necessarily mean agreeing with them;
b   studying differences in this way could lead to recognition that the best thing was to disagree amicably rather than to try and convert violently;
c   discussing how others worked and behaved could lead to a better understanding of ourselves. (from the diary of a teacher in School C)

This chapter will have given the reader some of the flavour of the Social Education Project both in terms of the assumptions made by project staff and the implications of acting upon these assumptions for the teacher. In the next chapter we turn to the reasons for introducing social education and the conditions that are necessary for its success.

VI. Implementing social education

In this chapter we discuss the reasons for introducing social education in schools, and illustrate this discussion with examples from the project schools. We shall begin by discussing certain common reactions of teachers who feel some anxiety about introducing social education. We shall go on to discuss how social education may be attempted in widely differing sorts of school organization. We conclude the chapter with a section on implications for team teaching, together with some general comments concerning other approaches to social education.

The information used in this chapter has been gathered from conversations with teachers in staff rooms in project schools, noted by ourselves or by the teachers of social education in project schools, from our work with the full-time teachers doing the one-year in-service diploma course at the University, and from work at teachers' centres and colleges of education. These teachers have raised the general questions with which we try to deal in the first part of the chapter. The information about the practical difficulties and opportunities of social education work has come from our own diaries on work in project schools, the diaries of teachers involved, interviews with project school teachers done as part of the evaluation, and from papers prepared for the Social Education working party, which consisted of teachers from the project schools and members of staff of Nottingham University School of Education.

1. Objections and replies

In the course of the project we became accustomed to four reactions from teachers who heard what we were trying to do. These reactions seemed to be based upon a number of doubts that require serious examination by the social educator.

The first reaction on hearing about the project may be paraphrased thus:

> What you propose to teach in social education is not something that ought to be made explicit. The school's task is to increase children's awareness of their social responsibilities through the way in which the school is organized and run, e.g. via house assemblies, prefect systems and pastoral care. The children then learn implicitly about belonging to a social institution and they pick up or reject its value system. It is not the task of the teacher to

105

explicitly examine the school as a social institution with a view to encouraging children to change relationships or structures.

This first reaction was voiced by a wide variety of schools and teachers. The project team does not deny the importance of implicit social learning. Indeed, it seems clear that almost everything which goes on in a school passes some message to the child. The way he is streamed, the mode of address used by teachers, the rewards and punishments system – all give the child some indication of how he is regarded. It seems to us essential for the teacher to recognize that this implicit learning is happening – and then to examine it.

One of our own project schools held that the main task of a teacher deeply interested in social education was to see that the school's philosophy was one that recognized that the main function of the school was to develop the child as a social being. Moreover, in an interesting paper, 'Some aspects of implicit social learning', a teacher from project School B argued convincingly that the real task of the social educator was to seek to secure certain forms of organization and ways of behaviour. For example, one should work for a rewards system that avoided house points and competitive exams, one which ensured the absence of corporal punishment and which recognized that anti-social behaviour is often a cry for help from an individual child in difficulty. The ideal system of discipline should be based on the proposition that self-discipline is the only goal worth striving for. It must therefore avoid regimentation through rules governing dress, movement around school, etc.

He went on to suggest that trying to work towards a non-streamed school not obsessed with examinations, based on a curriculum in which inquiry, not fact-learning, was stressed, and where opportunities for individual and group work were provided, would do much to ensure the right kind of social environment. Finally, the social educator should work for improved relationships and increased consultation and involvement with parents, youth leaders, welfare workers and organizations in the local community.

In one sense there can be no disagreement with the proposition that a child in such a school will probably develop satisfactorily as a social being. However, a number of qualifications were made by the project team and we feel that these justify our basic proposition that an *explicit* examination by children of the groups, the institution and the community to which they belong, is vital to children if they are to become aware of their community and its problems, identify with them and participate actively in their solution.

The first qualification is that the *implicit* approach is based on the assumption that a process of osmosis takes place in which the child recognizes the value of belonging to a caring community and understands what makes it so. Only an explicit examination – and the deliberate creation of opportunities for taking responsibility for changing things – can help children towards a realization that the groups to which they belong can be altered. Only an explicit examination can provide them with the skills to change situations. Interestingly, in School B a group of girls who were looking at what groups they belonged to complained that the process was painful because they belonged to different groups (skinheads and mods in this case), and divisions arose when sensitive topics were discussed. However, a central assumption of our work is that there is a need to recognize the causes of such divisions, and to learn how to resolve these, rather than glossing over any issue for fear that it might prove controversial.

In the second place, advocates of implicit social education assume an ideal school and an ideal community. Where these do not already exist, we are given no lead as to how they can be achieved, especially if the head or a substantial majority of staff do not share our scale of values. The explicit approach ensures that children and staff will be helped to work out the kinds of relationships and school which they want to exist and at the same time to recognize conflict situations and to handle them. It would perhaps be useful to illustrate this point by reference to an incident which occurred in School D.

At the centre of this particular story is a boy who had already been pointed out to us as a trouble-maker, and who was recognized by one of the project team as being in need of psychiatric help in his first year at the school. We had gone in to teach a session which was planned to open with a report from the class committee of an interview they had had with a visitor from the Schools Council. The extract from Wyn Williams' diary reads:

> When I attempted to start proceedings, the committee sat sullenly in their seats and refused to move or begin. John asked what had upset them. They refused to admit they were upset. 'All right, who has been beaten?', he asked. Immediately, the 'difficult' boy admitted that he had been beaten. He was on the committee. The class then began to mutter about the unfairness of the punishment – six strokes administered by the head.
>
> It appeared that the boy had hurt himself while doing gym. The class all supported this story. His response had been to get up and leave the gym – without permission and without explaining what had happened to the PE master. The latter had taken him to the head for punishment.

Of course, the incident itself cannot be isolated from this boy's frequent clashes with authority and his obsessive feelings of victimization. Asked why he had not asked permission of the master, he claimed that no notice would have been taken of him, whether or not he had genuinely been hurt. This was substantiated by a number of boys. However, there was one who remarked that by failing even to try to explain, he had put the PE master in a difficult situation and could hardly be surprised at the result. On being asked what they had done, the rest of the class said they had done nothing.

The social education teacher would have looked for a different outcome, as follows:

1   A socially educated boy would have attempted to make an explanation to his fellow pupils and to the teacher.
2   If the teacher failed to listen, the group would have put forward a case in support of him.
3   If the teacher still refused to listen, they would have accompanied both the teacher and the boy to the headmaster, when they would ask for permission to support his explanation.

This approach is obviously not an easy one, either for the teacher or for the class. But before rejecting it, one would need to show how else children can learn democracy if not by practising it. Moreover, where there is conflict to begin with, further conflict will ensue so long as no attempt is made in conclusion to resolve its causes. Because it involves children directly in the examination of their peer groups, school and community, social education has a more democratic basis than the attempt to secure staff co-operation in reforming the school from the top. There is also another danger in the implicit approach. It is based upon the concept that social education can be limited to the school. The Social Education Project's ultimate goal is active participation by the youngsters in the neighbourhood as well as the school.

The second reaction that we met from a number of teachers was that social education is no different in content from social studies, or thematic work done in English or RE, and no different in action from community service. What they were really saying here was that they were already doing social education, perfectly adequately, thus making a Schools Council project unnecessary. It must be admitted that work on outsiders and scapegoats, for instance, is sometimes done in English or integrated courses. But it is rarely done in the manner attempted in a social education course. One of the teachers in School B remarked in his diary that the course had definite possibilities as a 'new' approach to the theme. The newness lay in the attempt to enable groups not merely to identify scapegoats or outsiders, but to understand why groups develop the need for scapegoats, and to examine their own groups for symptoms of scapegoatism, with a view to countering it. This particular teacher got the class to relate jokes

108

they had heard which had a racial or religious bias, and then to find out why so many were hostile to particular groups of people. This was followed by an examination of various types of groups, and of the conditions in which scapegoatism thrives.

The normal approach to this kind of work involves the children in studies of particular minority groups in society, with the aim of raising their level of tolerance, and producing a liberal attitude. A danger here is that, even if successful, this approach will not enable young people to recognize symptoms of scapegoatism, and the first new minority group which appears on the scene could well suffer, even at the hands of those children who have the 'right' attitude towards the common minority groups.

This is not to say that certain social studies materials are of no use. Indeed, during the course of the project, many such were used, e.g. trial versions of the Keele Integrated Studies Project material on living in groups and the Humanities Project pack on relations between the sexes.* But in most cases, the material was used only as an initial stimulus or to illustrate the generality of a theme. Whenever possible it was supplemented by work which focused on the personal experiences of the pupils in their own groupings.

There is another aspect of approach to content that makes social education different from social studies.† Social studies work does not prescribe a specific role for the teacher; social education work does. A firm paternalist is often a lively and effective teacher of social studies, but in social education he is going to find it necessary consciously to adapt his role. The approach requires that he be a senior colleague with junior colleagues in a group that controls itself and determines its own programme. This does not mean that he cannot contribute nor that he may not make his presence felt. In fact, since we emphasize the value of conflict in helping to clarify the choices open to a group, the teacher has a dynamic role. This role is not, however, to determine independently the programme for the group, nor should the teacher alone decide on action arising from surveys done by the group.

The question of the kind of 'action' to be taken by the class brings us to a crucial distinction between social education and community service. In most cases, the choice of how to help the community and individuals within it is fairly clearly determined by the teacher in community service work. After all, he has

* Published as Schools Council Humanities Curriculum Project, *Relations Between the Sexes* (Heinemann Educational Books, 1970).

† For an account of the Schools Council's Social Studies Project see Schools Council Working Paper 39, *Social Studies 8–13*, by Denis Lawton, James Campbell and Valerie Burkitt (Evans/Methuen Educational, 1971).

the information on which to base a decision. He can then safely predict the outcome of the actions undertaken by the children. However, in social education the basis for taking a decision as to what, if anything, to do, is in the hands of the class who will have completed a preliminary action survey. From the teacher's personal point of view this can raise problems – as was described in the previous chapter.

Another comment needs to be made about social education and the question of content. The project examines themes or topics such as the family, the class, the school, the outsider, the scapegoat and the local community. What became increasingly clear was that the whole concept of the young 'urbanite', in terms of the problems faced and the skills required, might well be an area of study demanding much more consideration than either social studies courses or the Social Education Project itself had given it.

However, one final point needs to be made about the similarity of theme or topic between social education and social studies. The former assumes that the study of the family for a 13-year-old will be very different from the study of the family at 18. After all, the topic is explored because the family has a tremendous impact on the youngster, but the impact is different and the relationships are different at different times. Therefore, the nature of the content and the way in which it is explored arise from the class's interest. Thus, for example, 13-year-olds may well examine the extended family's supportive role while 18-year-olds examine how a change of status from school to work alters relationships. The remark by one teacher of a third-year class, that 'They did "The Family" in the first year' suggests a traditional social studies approach.

The third reaction to social education that we met from teachers was more negative. It was maintained that social education was a subversive agent in a school, seeking to disrupt the socializing process in which the school was involved by teaching its pupils an accepted pattern of social behaviour and values. There can be little doubt that of the three reactions mentioned this is most diametrically opposed to the assumption of social education. Social education cannot be equated with socialization defined in this way. Many teachers recognize that a school has at least two tasks to accomplish. One is to train children for their future careers; the other is to transmit the accumulated values of their society. The second of these two tasks is usually defined as 'socializing' the child. We wish to distinguish between the Social Education Project's approach and this definition of the dual role of the school. First, the project emphasized the role of the school as an agent of change as well as transmitter of values. Second, the project approach made explicit attempts to deal with social issues which are usually dealt with implicitly, if at all. Third, the project recognized the potency

110

which prevailing staff attitudes and organizational structures within a school have as agents of social learning for children. For instance, streaming tells the child that he is either better or worse than other children in the eyes of the school. We sought to challenge the validity of many of the assumptions underlying this implicit social learning and to offer alternatives. Social education implies a philosophy of education which lays stress upon certain propositions:

1 The proper teacher–pupil relationship is for the teacher to be adviser and experienced colleague and not mere dispenser of knowledge or arbiter of values.
2 The school's reward system and mode of grouping children must not emphasize failure or competition. It should rest on co-operative work among individuals and groups whose satisfaction lies not in obtaining house points or praise, but in the recognition by themselves and their peers that they have contributed to the task in hand.
3 An inquiry-based curriculum with individual and group research will sometimes result in action to change situations in school and community.
4 The school and community are integrally linked. The class is involved in the task of identifying ways in which school can be a supportive agency for change in the community.

If the first two of these are ignored, then the danger exists of a situation developing similar to one which occurred in the first year of the project, in one of the original project schools which was not retained. In this school, an attempt to explain that everyone could achieve success by developing his abilities was rudely interrupted by one boy: 'You don't understand the system, Sir.' 'All right, you explain it to me.' 'Well, Sir, at 11 we have to take a test, and the bright ones go to the grammar schools, then the dunces come here.' (Much amusement shown here.) 'Yes, Sir,' said another, 'and when we are here in this school, they divide the clever dunces and put them in the A form, and the Bs . . .' 'And,' said another boy, 'we're the D. We're the dustbin.' This caused a roar of laughter.

In our view, this story illustrates perfectly the dangerous effects that school organization can have upon children's views of themselves. They had perceived how others rated them and they had accepted it in the sense that they had no intention of making any effort beyond that needed to stay out of trouble. Attempts in the fourth year to remedy this situation with 'Newsom' schemes or social education programmes are unlikely to have much effect, not because of the inadequacy of the methods, but because it is too late. That the last two of these four propositions are realistic can be seen from the work described in Chapter II.

The fourth reaction of teachers was that children of secondary-school age, particularly from the lower streams, were not capable of doing this kind of work. Thus a teacher in his evaluation interview (July 1970), commenting upon the work we were trying to do (with a fourth-year streamed group of leavers), stated: 'I think if this kind of work is done with children whose IQ is higher you can well have marvellous success, but one has got to remember all the time that we are dealing with the lower IQ range.'

He was talking about a class which handled a twenty-minute discussion about what they understood by the words 'a crowd', 'a democratic group' and 'a paternalistic group'. The pupils gave examples and were able to identify the types of group thus identified in the BBC film *Last Bus*. They had to recognize a 'crowd' situation and a 'paternalistic boss group' at work. By dramatization they then illustrated how different group responses could lead to changes of situation. Of this class the same teacher was later able to say that he was 'amazed' at their ability to understand the concept of types of groups and could see the high degree of involvement.

This story illustrates one of our major assumptions. The work we do in social education is readily within the grasp of all children, whatever their level of ability. The problem which this teacher illustrated lies in the expectations that teachers have of children and their ability to communicate complex thoughts about social interaction. It is apparent that children come to accept a different and better view of their own abilities when the teachers themselves do not lack faith in them.

2. Introducing social education into the curriculum

The teacher who accepts the need for an explicit programme of social education will need to be aware of the kinds of reactions likely to be provoked by his attempt. Introducing social education in a school organized upon basic assumptions which run contrary to those stated above is obviously going to be difficult. Even within our project schools, two incidents illustrate the issues involved. An argument took place between one of the project staff and the deputy headteacher about a child who was chewing gum in a class which he was conducting. In the argument which followed the deputy head expressed the view that (a) it was her responsibility to maintain discipline, and (b) the teaching of social education was undermining discipline by giving 'too much freedom to the children'.

In another school, the head refused to show a film on the grounds that it showed four boys not paying their bus fare and that this would set a bad example to pupils.

Both incidents stem from the sense of responsibility felt by all teachers for the behaviour of the children in their care. They reflect a direct conflict with our assumption that the development of self-discipline depends upon providing situations in which contentious issues will emerge, rather than impressing on children what is right or wrong.

This conflict over the role of the school may result in the emergence in the staff of groups who are hostile to social education. They have been categorized in a paper written by a teacher in School A who listed four such groups:

1   authoritarians who may feel threatened by the freedom of expression of the pupils and by the pupil–teacher exchanges which are essential to our conception of social education;

2   strongly subject-oriented teachers who may be anxious about parts of the syllabus which may be 'missed' if time is given over to social education;

3   those whose discipline is weak, who feel even less secure when they come into contact with pupils who are used to expressing themselves fairly freely (clearly, there is a temptation for pupils to exploit this situation);

4   teachers anxious about the reputation of the school who fear that pupils may let the school down when they are allowed out of school unsupervised.

The writer advises the teacher embarking on a programme of social education to explain right from the start what he wishes to do, as well as the consequences that may follow. Above all, he must try to ensure some measure of success in the early stages. He suggests that support from outside (for instance from colleges of education or universities) may help in giving status to social education work.

It is clear, then, that in social education the teacher needs to prepare for the stages through which pupils pass when encouraged to challenge and question. Children who have not been used to freedom can hardly be expected to handle it easily when it is granted. The first reaction may well be some form of aggression. If this is met with a simple return to corrective discipline, then children may never learn to handle freedom. If the teacher is prepared for this reaction, and shows that he is, understanding and acceptance will eventually follow. Only then will pupils gain the ability to handle freedom.

The teacher will also need to raise with the children the implication of his approach for their relationship with other teachers. Finally, the social education teacher must discuss what he is doing with his colleagues and explain the assumptions upon which it is based. Such discussions give him the opportunity to examine his own assumptions, as well as those which underlie the school's philosophy. They will help to determine what will be his best strategy for introducing social education.

Just as it is important to prepare the ground by winning over other members of staff to the aims of social education, so the actual work of the pupils must be seen as a continuous programme. The more ambitious ventures can only be undertaken when the basic skills have been acquired and when the pupils have gained enough in responsibility and initiative. The class with which to start social education ought not to be the fourth-year leavers. A second-year class can be worked with over a three-year period; fourth-years attempting social education have neither learnt the necessary skills, nor handled, in most cases, the responsibility for planning, organizing and presenting their own work. The importance of continuity to this work over a considerable period of time cannot be overstated. If social education is regarded as a stop-gap for an early-leavers' course, or as a palliative for early-leavers, it cannot but fail. The skills which pupils need to carry out the more sophisticated stages of a social education programme cannot be developed overnight. Social education is a process. It is not a question of applying a syllabus knowing that there will be certain results. Flexibility is essential, since different classes will react in very different ways to similar stimuli or opportunities.

During the course of the project it was in School A, which carried the work through with the same pupils throughout the final two years of the project, that pupils experienced the deepest level of involvement. School C, so successful in many ways, did not reach the final goal, partly because they had not had sufficient time in the preliminary stages. Not the least cause of the lack of involvement in School D was the fact that the pupils in the social education group changed so drastically. This meant that very few had undergone a full course of social education, and the majority were unable to experience the continuity of the process. The earlier the process is begun, the earlier it can come to fruition. Much of the preliminary work could be attempted in primary schools, and certainly in the first year of secondary schooling.

This catalogue of difficulties may seem somewhat overwhelming to the teacher considering a social education approach. It should not do so. As must be obvious from the fact that the project team was able to carry out their work in these project schools, there are a considerable number of teachers who feel the relevance of the social education approach, and it is to them that such a teacher must turn in the early stages.

It is worth concluding this section by recalling that our assumptions about the proper relationships that ought to exist between teacher and pupils are not unique. Many schools are based on such assumptions and it is interesting that in the one project school where this was conspicuously true, the approach of social education was welcomed as reinforcing rather than threatening or under-

114

mining the assumptions of the school. It reinforced the encouragement the school gave to 'kids to express themselves more than we have ever allowed them to do before, particularly on the grounds of questioning other people's standards and attitudes'; and secondly, it encouraged the school to make explicit an implicit philosophy on which the school was run. Even in schools where teacher–pupil relationships are more traditional, favourable changes have been noted in the attitude of children to teachers involved in social education.

3. Introducing social education: maximum or minimum level

Not all schools, or teachers within them, are likely to be faced with the ideal situation for introducing social education. It is therefore necessary to consider the different levels at which it may be introduced.

At a minimum level, the main preoccupation of the teacher of social education needs to be his/her colleagues. The main aim is to get them to discuss and argue about the objectives of social education as a philosophy before an attempt is made to get them to become involved in any social education work.

The minimum requirements for introducing social education are one teacher, time on the timetable and a class to teach. Even this requires careful examination, for one teacher attempting social education on his own runs the risk with his class of being chosen as scapegoat for everything that ails the school. Social education groups making a noise in other lessons have been greeted with 'You are not doing social education now', and complaints about undermining discipline have been levelled at teachers involved in two of the schools. Given such reactions, it is vital for a teacher proposing to do social education to estimate which of the staff would find the approach to children impossible to accept and to talk to them about possible difficulties and how they can be overcome.

Asking for time on the timetable is another difficulty to be thought about. Two periods a week on a timetable is quite unsuited to social education work. The topic or themes that are examined usually require an intensive short-term effort rather than a weekly dose. For example, in School C the school profile involved ten periods a week over a six-week period. Similarly, a study of the generation gap involved four sessions of planning followed by a half-term's work for three periods a week. In School A the attempt to cram the survey work involved in an examination of a redevelopment scheme into two periods meant spreading the work over one-and-a-half terms, with all the frustrations of not being able to achieve a rapid end-product. Far more time is needed to implement a project of this kind. When it is being planned or when it is already completed, the discussions can be contained within an allocation of a few short periods.

115

At a maximum level, the social education teacher is merely one of a staff who already accept the objectives of this project. His role is to work on *explicit* schemes to examine the community of the school and its relationship with the neighbourhood community. Almost certainly he will be a member of a team, and social education in the explicit sense will be done as and when staff and pupils see fit to examine social issues in school or in the area, and take action concerning them.

4. Co-operative teaching

In all the project schools the social education teachers at some point became involved in teams. Given the themes which they were encouraged to attempt, the opportunities for team work abound. The composition of such teams varied in the four schools:

A   included mathematics, geography, English and woodwork;
B   included history, geography, English, art and RE;
C   included a group of humanities teachers;
D   included geography, music, English and mathematics.

Not only did the composition of teams vary. So did the success with which they worked. In School A, as described earlier, the team in year 2 never really became one. A small group of three teachers actively pursued social education, while other teachers were seen as resource agents who would contribute when asked to do so in specific areas, e.g. a geographical study of the district. The weaknesses apparent in this situation – a tendency for resource agents to feel that they were being used and to resent it, and for those most involved to feel that the latter put their social education commitment last – led to the team leader's comment that the team's effort was an example of how *not* to do social education.

In School C, teams in the humanities are a regular feature of school life and, therefore, the project was highly successful in terms of team-teaching. However, lack of feedback from the groups in the fourth year was given as one reason why the school profile was less satisfactory than an individual class profile had been.

'With four forms working at the same time on the profile much interesting discussion is missed by too many of the forms.' This interesting comment from a teacher recognizes the fact that team-teaching involves pupils as well as teachers. Solving the problems of teacher communication is not enough in itself.

In School B the decision to co-operate in social education led to independent work by a number of teachers. The result was that pupils began to complain that they were doing social education in every lesson! Our insistence on the importance of social education does not mean that we believe that it ought to dominate everything else. Mere repetition is counterproductive.

116

In School D, the attempt to organize the whole of the fourth year on a survey of the village was doomed from the beginning. There was no understanding of aims and objectives among the staff team, no idea of their exact function in the survey, and no skills among the children in interviewing, and collating and presenting information.

Comments on how to operate successfully in the team situation now abound as a result of work in IDE (interdisciplinary enquiry work) by Goldsmiths' College Curriculum Laboratory).

In social education, the successful team is likely to need to:

a   plan carefully ahead – at least 4 or 5 weeks before starting a topic or a theme;

b   involve children straightaway in the suggestions about what information is required, what the objectives are and how they are to be achieved;

c   regard the team as one whole, rather than several specialists, each contributing his own specialized knowledge (this is not to say that specialized knowledge is irrelevant – there will be occasions when many classes can benefit from any one man's expertise);

d   remember that each team is different. It must find its own salvation – learning from its own mistakes.

5. Summary

1. Social education is not a 'subject' – rather it is an explicit attempt to examine and create social situations so that children can become aware of problems, identify with their groups and seek ways to act in solving these problems.

This means that (a) time is needed fairly regularly (say two periods a week) for the skills of observation and communication to be developed; (b) time in large blocks is needed when skills are applied to a particular issue, e.g. a school profile or a study of the generation gap.

2. Social education assumes role-changes on the part of teachers and pupils which will prove extremely difficult for some staff to accept. It can never be entirely satisfactorily done by one person on the staff without at least the sympathy of a number of colleagues. Before starting the work, there must be constant dialogue with colleagues and children, and a willingness to recognize the possibility and even inevitability of conflict. In particular it is vital that teachers realize that children are being asked to do two things: to challenge and question; and to adjust their behaviour in recognition of their increased responsibility. In reality these two do not always go hand in hand. The first is more likely to come easily to them.

3. For teacher and pupils alike, social education creates opportunities for the development of insight into themselves and their interrelationships. The opportunities arise partly from the explicit attempt to create greater self-awareness and group solidarity. They also arise from discussions of mistakes which may be made. Mistakes cannot be avoided, but they can be turned to profit.

But, of course, it is not only mistakes that provide opportunities. Thus through her work on the project, a teacher who once required absolute silence in her classroom came to recognize that involved groups of children working together on a task make some noise. Previously she had feared socio-drama because it was noisy. She became the most expert teacher at using the technique. This development arose from her willingness to try a new approach because of its opportunities and her gradual adjustment to all its consequences.

The example which occurred in School B was paralleled in other schools too. Given preparation, anticipation, willingness to learn from errors and willingness to change, social education can succeed. When it does, success breeds more success.

VII. Conclusions and recommendations

1. Social education should be seen as a process which begins early in a child's secondary-school career, or even in the primary school, and continues right the way through it. The description of the process given in Chapter II involves children doing observation and communication work throughout their secondary-school career. Much of this work can be done within the framework of an existing subject-based timetable, particularly in the humanities. It ought to be linked fairly early on to profiles of the type described in Chapter II.

It is not desirable to see social education merely as a way of getting school-leavers out of school in their final year. Without the firm basis of skill-training before the final year, this can only lead to frustration and confusion.

2. Social education must be made an *explicit* process. It is not enough to leave children to the implicit social education conveyed by the way in which the school is organized and the way in which teachers speak to them, i.e. in the organization and 'tone' of a school. It is vital to make the process explicit because by doing so we bring home to children the idea that it is *their* opportunity to examine the groups and organizations to which they belong, and that it is *their* job to seek changes if changes are needed. An explicit process also recognizes that certain skills need to be developed if the ability to control our environment is really to be effective.

3. The fact that this project was concerned with the less able child in non-selective schools does not mean that social education is only for the 'Newsom' child. The basic principle of social education – that everyone needs to develop the skills to examine, challenge and control his immediate situation in school and community – is a principle that ought to be applied in every school in the country, and for the children of all (so-called) levels of ability. What must not happen, however, is the takeover of social education by sixth forms and upper streams, as has so often happened to other schemes, such as the Duke of Edinburgh Award Scheme.

4. The type of social education defined in this report is based upon an assumption that the secondary school as it exists is ill-adapted to its function as a socializing agent in our society. We argue that education should encourage an awareness of the social environment and the ability on the part of individuals and groups to effect changes. Basically, social education of this type is dependent upon a relationship between pupil and teacher which is democratic. They are colleagues, jointly seeking answers to questions about the problems and challenges of the immediate school and community. Responsibility for control in the classroom is shifted gradually from being principally that of the teacher to a joint responsibility of teacher and children.

Our recommendation is that, in the classroom, teachers should deliberately create situations in which children take decisions. Children must work together in groups and increasingly determine both *what* they examine and *how* they do it.

This transfer of some of the teacher's power means greater responsibility being taken by children. They will need to go out of school unsupervised. They will need to determine what problems they choose to tackle and how they will examine them. Finally, they will have to determine what kinds of action, if any, need to be carried out.

This implies not an abdication of the teacher's responsibility, but a change in his role. These are new and positive functions for the teacher to fulfil.

He must have a function as an adult examining proposals for action and foreseeing snags and difficulties.

He must examine priorities. How much time would be involved in following up and supporting any given action? Can colleagues and head be persuaded that it is legitimate?

5. When children are given their heads, the teacher must learn to recognize a whole new series of symptoms of success. For example, when a child begins to question decisions which affect him, not from an adolescent anti-authority standpoint but as a sign of an awakening concern for wider issues, his behaviour may be registered as a 'success'. The same questioning might point to a breakdown of teacher–pupil relationships in a traditional school.

6. Social education at a minimum level can be attempted in a school by one teacher with one class with an allocation of two periods a week. Those two periods may be used for observation and training in communication skills. However, he will need to persuade colleagues to agree to a fairly intensive treatment when constructing a profile – say, six periods a week for a short period of time.

Social education should not be started with the fourth year unless everything

120

else has failed. If a start is made with the fourth year, it is better to start with a profile in school which will allow the development of the necessary skills before attempting work outside.

Colleagues should *always* be involved – at least by starting discussions in the staff room about the objectives of social education and its possible implications. Especially necessary is the need to explain that children may challenge and question other teachers' decisions.

Teachers find it much easier to respond to new suggestions when they know what the underlying assumptions are and what their implications are.

7. A social education programme seeks to produce youngsters who are actively involved in their community. It cannot predict, and even deliberately avoids predicting, what kind of action they will seek to take. On occasions they may decide to do nothing about a situation which the teacher thinks ought to be changed. On other occasions they will suggest actions in which the teacher feels he is not competent to assist, or in which assistance on his part would be wrong.

This conclusion about action leads us to recommend that teachers and pupils in the last year especially should have time to follow up decisions which they seek to implement. There is a need for far more time in the last year for teachers and pupils alike to be free to become involved in the community.

We would recommend that schools embarking on explicit social education programmes recognize that at least one member of staff must be given the time to establish contacts in the community and must receive as much school support as possible in relation to the outside community.

8. Since social education is seen as a process, it is obviously better for a teacher to have a continuing relationship with a group of children undergoing this process. Thus it is recommended that teachers have regular contact with groups of children over two, three or four years.

This may be facilitated by having teams of teachers, responsible for groups of subjects on the curriculum, who move up the school with a year group. Class teachers, house tutors or year tutors moving up the school with a class would similarly help to establish the desired relationships.

9. Opportunities for revaluation by children and staff of themselves and each other arise from the open-ended situations that abound in social education. Mistakes will be made. It is essential for teachers to recognize that occasional panic over this situation is common and benign. As one teacher put it, 'Sometimes I just want to get them all back behind their desks and have some peace.' This is

121

a perfectly normal reaction and one for which he ought to be prepared. It is also essential to recognize that mistakes often constitute further opportunities to learn. Clearly, this demands structures within which teachers can participate in ongoing discussions about their work. This is why we recommend team-teaching as being the kind of approach most likely to facilitate the effective implementation of the work.

10. If a serious attempt is to be made to involve the community including, inevitably, parents – there must be provision for one or more 'community rooms'. These would be at the disposal of parents and residents as a base for community projects initiated in conjunction with teachers and children.

While this may be most appropriately established in a purpose-built section of a school, alteration of, or dual use of, existing rooms may be feasible alternatives.

11. One of the clearest results of the evaluation was that social education work offers an opportunity for children to develop talents and skills of which they and their teachers were unaware.

This means three things. First, the child is encouraged by his success, and will wish to make further efforts. Second, the teacher's expectations of his children will rise and this will have a further positive impact upon them. Third, it means that the teacher must not 'spoon-feed' children by over-preparation of materials and ideas. Concentration on the production of teacher-proof kits may well result in child-proof kits. That is to say, there will be no scope left for the initiative of the child.

Appendices

Appendix A Project discussion papers

1. An Experiment in Social Education: Social Topography*

Social topography is the study of an area in terms of its organizations, its structures and social services; that is how these affect, for example, single persons, the life of families and of the neighbourhood, the peer groups (groups of equals) or the special sub-cultures: both the concrete and visible conditions and the invisible ones and the special attitudes and mentality surrounding these concrete conditions – what is called the 'social climate'. One of the main aims of such a study is to discover what exists to meet the requirements of the local population on a basis of its groups. For instance:

> What is being done in area X for babies and young mothers?
> What is there for children of three to primary-school age, for children of secondary-school age?
> What happens to them from fifteen onwards (to, say, twenty) once they have left school?
> What are the needs of the young marrieds?
> Where do people meet one another?
> What are the specific needs of the middle-aged and the elderly? (This category includes both those who, however advanced their age, can still perform the daily acts of living, and also those who have some handicap which hinders them from eating, washing, collecting what needs to be collected, etc.)

Analysing findings on a basis of age groups

CHILDREN

1. Places to play.
2. Different kinds of parks and gardens; playgrounds, indoor rooms for play, recreation, homework.

* Discussion paper provided for the project by Richard Hauser of the Centre for Group Studies.

123

3. What kind of entertainments are there for passive enjoyment and what kind of amenities for sports? Again and again we find that places for sport exist which the youngsters are not allowed to make use of unless accompanied by a parent or a teacher, neither of whom is likely to be available after school, on Saturdays, Sundays or during the holidays.

4. 'Latch-key' children constitute a particular problem. In some areas they comprise as much as 70 per cent of their age group. That mothers go out to work is one of the chief characteristics of British working-class life today, due to workers receiving a low wage, and making up with overtime, special perks and their wives' pay. In addition to economic reasons, many women want to go out to work because they are bored at home, particularly in New Towns. Whether we like it or not, there are latch-key children, many of whose mothers are not only away at work when the children come home from school but whose mothers leave for work before the children leave for school. Some mothers deposit quite young children in the school playground as much as an hour before school starts – which is not much fun in winter. These children's special needs should be examined and catered for.

YOUNG PEOPLE

1. Places in which to get together and have intelligent discussions and possibly action.

2. Many young people today want to get away to enjoy themselves. Having motorbikes makes them mobile enough to want to have their centres and meeting places well away from home and mother. The police in Manchester did a survey for me [Richard Hauser] and for themselves which revealed that the youngsters from Moss Side (which is a kind of Soho-cum-Notting Hill Gate) leave the area to have their fun, while other youngsters from somewhere else come in to Moss Side to have theirs.

3. Is it not becoming reasonable, as well as desirable, to build community centres away from home? Biggin Hill is a successful and popular example.

4. And what are the chances for courting couples? All respectable communities have a lovers' lane.

5. Youth organizations in general should be examined in their formal as well as in their informal aspects. We have found certain pubs and improvised meeting places which are *de facto* youth clubs. There is no opportunity whatever for the training of youth leaders who will cater for the needs of the 'Newsom' children. The need for such leadership is overwhelming since Newsom children comprise 50 per cent of their age group. The situation is

124

absolutely scandalous, but nobody bothers about it since these people's sub-culture does not function on an organized or conscious basis, and they are therefore unable to constitute a pressure group in their own right.

ADULTS

1. Places where middle-aged and older people can get together and do something of social value to the community, if they are stimulated to do so, as well as have fun, etc.
2. If such facilities exist, where are they?
3. Are different kinds of facilities needed or available for summer and in winter?
4. Places where the cultural heritage should be available and developed for all ages – theatres, concert halls, art galleries, libraries, etc.

Working mothers
It is wrong to blame the parents whether, as in some cases, they simply need the extra money, or, being subject to all the pressures of society, they conform to certain stereotypes: every family in the street has a car of a certain type, or a washing machine, or a cocktail cabinet, or some other thing, depending on the level at which they live, for which the wife must produce the money because the husband's earnings cannot stretch that far.

The social topography of an area includes knowledge of its various incomes and social strata, which are likely to be in a constant state of flux.

The Church
Another frame of reference is the Church. What part does it play?

One must admit, regretfully, that the Church is not producing the values it ought to or could produce. I refer, of course, to community values, not religious ones. Whenever I train priests and ministers I say to them that in their *religious* role they may be shepherds of their flock; but in their community role they are only senior sheep. There is no question of their having any priority over others, and if they cannot see it in this way, they will achieve nothing. Yet I would say that it is necessary to try and find out objectively what goes on within the Church structure, its youth organizations, old people's organizations and so on. Some parsons are extremely good in this respect, but unfortunately most of them are of no use as community workers.

The work situation
Where do people work? Do they work in their area or do they have to seek work outside it?

125

In Manchester some people travel as much as fifteen miles from their New Towns to their old places of work because their friends are there and there may be no work in the New Towns anyway. This is extremely expensive and harassing.

We must investigate the work situation of the youngsters, the women and the elderly as well. What are the facilities for further training, if any? The question of apprenticeships is a very complex and uncertain one today because they are still given along traditional lines, in more and more of a vacuum, divorced from genuine work opportunities. Many present-day apprentices will in future – though perhaps not immediately – be made redundant and find their skills obsolete because of automated machinery which will be so much better able to perform the tasks than any skilled man.

The neighbourhood

Ideally a neighbourhood consists of people who are near enough to see each other daily (like a small village of say 2000 to 3000 people – supporting a primary school of 300).

Does it have a natural centre for meeting? Is there a centre where all ages can meet?

What is the strength of the *neighbourhood loyalties*? The best way to find out is to ask what would happen to the children if their mothers were sick. There are 14 000 children in this country in short-term care (up to six weeks) for no other reason than that there are no neighbours or family members prepared or able to take the child or children in. What should be done about this?

Similarly, what happens to the old people when they become dependent? This question also provides a criterion of neighbourhood loyalties.

The community

Is there a community to which people feel loyal? How strong is this loyalty?

Does the community consist of different neighbourhoods which are clearly defined? Have these neighbourhoods their own factual and invisible character? Has the community?

How far are the institutions really run by the community leaders? What are the administrative services in the area? Who carries the main technical burdens for the community? Which service is known to do this well? Which service is known to do this not so well?

Newcomers

Are there any newcomer groups? What happens to newcomers? Are they helped to settle in, and by whom? Are they welcome or not? If either, why?

Sub-cultures, minorities, scapegoats

One must also investigate the question of scapegoats, acting on the assumption that scapegoats exist. Nearly every community contains a percentage of particularly unpopular people. Who are they? Are they genuinely obnoxious or do they merely have a different culture from the majority? Do they tend to sing and dance, for instance? Perhaps they smell of garlic (which is an un-British smell)? Or is it some characteristic so completely different that it sets them apart from the rest of the community, and thus, most important of all, causes a loss of status among those who live next door to them? If I were from the lower middle class, my status would go down if a coloured man lived or worked next to me. On the other hand, I would be pleased if I worked next to a Jew, because the Jew would not work there if it were not a good job. If, however, I were from the upper middle class, and lived in the stockbroker belt, I would be delighted if the Maharajah of Timbuktu, or a foreign diplomat became my neighbour. If, on the other hand, my new neighbour were a Jew, I would be anxious, lest he lower the tone of the neighbourhood. In other words, in this particular social context, the scapegoats – to minor degrees of course – would be the Jews. In another context, where working-class security is at stake (and it is the secure working class which is gradually becoming middle class), the coloured man is the scapegoat.

Who *are* the local scapegoats, and why is the community looking for scapegoats, apart from finding someone to blame for annoying behaviour?

To find out whether the desire for scapegoats is independent of the stigmatized group, it is necessary to study the quality of tensions affecting majority culture and minority culture (or sub-culture). Are these tensions the results of real cultural differences? To what extent may they be due to the social underdevelopment of the parties involved?

A good example of minority or sub-culture is provided by the gipsies, or by a particularly aggressive type of young gang. The approach to them ought not to be entirely geographical.

How do the members of a particular sub-culture fare generally? What is their inner morale, their mentality? What are their taboos and value systems? Do they help each other? Is their social cohesiveness strong? What is their community life, their family life, their home life? What help can they give others, and what help do they need? Are they in any way dangerous to others, and are others in any way dangerous to them?

These are the lines on which the investigation of a sub-culture should proceed. It may be a local sub-culture, i.e. gangs, or it may be a regional or national sub-culture, i.e. coloureds, studied from a local point of view.

127

Politics

What organizations exist and do not exist (e.g. compared with other areas)? How far do people participate in local politics and national politics? How effective is the contact between political leaders and their voters? What community organizations exist to take special care of local programmes?

Danger areas

These are areas which give rise to the majority of mental health problems and crime problems owing to a static environment of social underdevelopment. Society usually waits for a complete breakdown to occur in such areas before rushing in. Moreover, the help it offers is always on an individual basis which leaves the contaminated areas as such untouched – an approach both dishonest and irrelevant.

When things go wrong, what happens to people who have to go to: the local hospital, the mental hospital, institutions for the sub-normal or physically handicapped, old people's homes, or homes for children? And what happens to those who are homeless, or in trouble with the law – young people or adults?

What happens if a youngster misbehaves?

How are the police and welfare services working?

How are public and private transport facilities affecting people's daily lives?

Evaluating the spirit of an institution

Of existing institutions, which are statutorily run and which are set up and run by the people themselves? What is the spirit in which they are functioning?

It must be borne in mind that however democratic the original ideal on which any institution was founded, it must not be taken for granted that this will never change. Take, for instance, the club originally built by the miners themselves in a number of mining villages and now used for drinking only. In effect, it is no more than a pub, and far from fulfilling the socially activating intention of its founders. All these are questions of social topography.

Synthesis

Once a social topography investigation has been carried out along the lines suggested, the character of the area begins to emerge, and an analysis made on this basis can take on some real significance.

We must now ask ourselves: how can analysis become synthesis, and what is to be done?

The important factor here is not what outsiders think the people in the neighbourhood or community *ought* to do – be they young or old or of whatever

128

group – but what the persons themselves want to do. If they have participated in the social topography they will no doubt have learned much about conditions they didn't know before; especially about the apathy (or sometimes the violence) of people (if conditions are wrong or unjust or hurtful) who feel unable to act ('What can I (or we) do on my (our) own?'). The answer is: 'Plenty', but only if:

(1) you feel indignant enough, strong enough, to want to act;
(2) you want to learn what can be done about it *intelligently* – to make this a really good plan;
(3) you are willing to get together and pull together and not to give up even if things go wrong;
(4) you are prepared to elect your leaders for action.

Sometimes you may already hold a very strong opinion of what is wrong. Please check it carefully – maybe you were misinformed, or you may discover previously unsuspected facts while carrying out a general social topography survey of your community, so that you will not live blindly and dumbly next to people who may need your help desperately. Social action is normally incomparably easier when carried out by a determined group – as against a number of single people.

But it is perfectly clear that no local survey makes any sense if people just sit back and complain. Often you will find, if you go into any mental hospital in your area, or any general hospital, or any institution for the subnormal, that there are desperate staffing problems. An ex-matron from an old people's home once told me that she had left because there were 'old ladies, many of them no longer compos mentis, or physically fit, who needed to be turned over every few hours in their beds, and we simply did not have the manpower to do it. They are being shot dead as surely as soldiers in battle, except that nobody knows about it, and nobody cares either.' Nor is this as extreme a case as people would like to think.

The main object in social topography, therefore, after gathering information and discovering problems, is to get local action going by the people themselves. 'What can WE do?' should be the first consideration all along and 'WE' are not you or I as influence leaders who have instigated the survey but the power leaders emerging from the group itself, the group of people discovered through the social topography survey, who are willing and interested to take responsibility for their area.

Most people have never become fully aware of their basic need to stick together; many have never learnt that it is necessary not only to *take* security and human warmth but equally to *give* them to others, through their efforts over and

129

above their minimum duty, i.e. not breaking the law. These would include such things as not throwing litter about, but would also go beyond making little gestures just for the sake of praise.

Life is so much richer if one cares enough for people to be bothered to find out what goes on in their daily lives, how they can be helped in a group or groups to change not small symptoms but the conditions of life. Doing this in and with groups and doing it for all those who are in a particular predicament, not just for one or two one happens to know, is to show true responsibility – as a true human being. To do this is right, nor must you forget the places of joy and of human warmth – this too must be part of your life. We must all go on growing throughout our lives, not just in youth. There, too, you and your groups will achieve satisfaction in so far as you show genuine concern for others and for other groups.

2. SUMMARY STATEMENT OF AIMS OF THE PROJECT

1. The principal aim of the project is 'to provide an enabling process through which children will achieve a sense of identification with their community, become sensitive to its shortcomings and develop methods of participation in those activities needed for the solution of social problems'. The final goal of the project is therefore to promote in young people an active interest in the affairs of their community.

2. An active interest presupposes social understanding, self-reliance and social skills. These are also aims in their own right.

3. Understanding of social structures is at once a prerequisite for the aims already stated, and an aim in itself. The aim of social education is a practical one. Any sub-structure may be relevant at any given time. Hence, we include in our aims awareness of different structures and recognition of social situations in which any particular structure is relevant.

4. We exclude any rigorous examination of the organization of social structures. Both institutions and persons participate in several structures. Hence they have many roles. Social education is not concerned to formalize the relations between roles. It is concerned with the understanding of social roles – in particular awareness of different roles, and of the sources of social conflict. This points to the need for understanding people, and the effect this has on role behaviour.

130

5. Since gain in understanding oneself comes from gain in understanding others, self-understanding is a further aim. It is widely held that self-understanding brings self-acceptance. There is some truth in this. In any event, self-acceptance is an objective, and may be achieved as the outcome of involvement as well as of self-understanding. Because of their measurability, it is as well to itemize at least two aspects of self-acceptance: setting realistic goals, and similarity of 'perceived self' and 'ideal self'.

6. Since an active interest in community affairs is the ultimate aim, social initiative is directly relevant. It is not merely an aid to understanding or to self-acceptance. Social initiative is a personality factor, so wide individual differences will remain, regardless of educational experience. Nevertheless, it is believed that the individual can learn to increase his potential for participation by the acquisition of social skills. As in the case of social understanding, it is possible to itemize a number of distinct educational objectives within the field of social skills:

(a) willingness to approach others;
(b) willingness to ask relevant questions and ability to do so;
(c) avoidance of off-putting questions and remarks;
(d) willingness to insert questions and remarks designed to put people at their ease;
(e) lack of undue inhibitions – willingness and ability to answer relevant and simple questions about self;
(f) making practical suggestions to initiate group action;
(g) accepting such suggestions from others;
(h) collaborating in group projects;
(i) leadership in group projects.

3. Guide to Profile Studies

The class profile

AIMS

1 To improve basic skills of observation and communication (e.g. looking and listening, writing, speaking, describing, etc.).
2 To enable children to understand the structure and significance of the various groups within the class.
3 To enable children to learn the skills and techniques required later for more advanced profiles of the school and community.

4   To enable children to have a clear understanding of the duties and respon-
     sibilities of themselves and their fellows.

    The profile sheet reproduced opposite is in no way meant to be a blueprint
to be followed slavishly. It is intended merely as a guide to groups of teachers to
enable them to select items and aspects of the profile which are particularly
appropriate to the needs of their children. It is recognized that some of the items
would inevitably be omitted by some schools; that different items would receive
different degrees of emphasis in different schools; and that teachers would wish to
include many of their own ideas which have not been included on our sample
sheet.
    Clearly, a school which uses team-teaching methods would have an organiza-
tional advantage over schools whose timetables are subject-based. However,
since subject-based timetables are more common, some guidance has been given
as to which areas of the timetable could viably be used for various aspects of the
profile. Once again, these are not arbitrary subject divisions, and no doubt
schools would wish to move these items into subject areas more appropriate
to their own particular interests and needs. It can be seen that many items have
been included more than once in different subject areas. This is because many
items can be considered from more than one point of view and underlines
the different emphases schools might wish to place on different aspects of the
profile.
    Many different methods have been used to teach various items of the profile
and no attempt has been made here to describe them or even to say which has
been most effective. This is because it is felt that teachers will be more effective if
they apply their own methods, and one conclusion that we have been able to
draw from observing different approaches to the school profile is that there are
many effective methods. So many external factors affect the teaching – e.g. the
relationship between staff and pupils, age and attitudes of pupils, the facilities in
the school, etc., and, perhaps above all, the needs of the children – that it would
be invidious to spell out *the* method. It is true to say, however, that children
working in small groups, with each group studying one aspect of the profile, has
proved effective. This is particularly true if they are allowed to suggest the
various items to be studied as a class, then to choose their own group and aspect
of study.
    Experience has shown that children have obtained great benefit from putting
on an exhibition of the completed school profile. It has given them a sense of
achievement, especially when other classes have been brought in to see the
exhibition. Furthermore, it has given different groups a more coherent picture of

132

SUGGESTED CLASS PROFILE

Suggested areas of teaching	Physical	Personality	Home	School	Out of school
Mathematics	Height and weight, averages, measuring			Timetable, dinners; teachers (distribution)	
English	Written descriptions; autographs	Accents; socio-drama of group interaction	Socio-drama of family conflict	School teams, clubs; socio-drama; written descriptions	Leisure-time activities, likes and dislikes; youth clubs, scouts, etc.; socio-drama of peer-group life
History/Geography	Birthplaces	Accents	Distance from school; family tree	Catchment area; relationship with primary school	Holidays
Art/Music	Life-size models and posters of average boy and girl; colouring of hair, eyes, etc.		Homes, décor, planning	Uniform	Hobbies, likes and dislikes; favourite music, etc.
Biology/Science	Fingerprints, photographs, hair samples		Siblings; ages of parents		
Needlecraft/Handicraft	See art				Hobbies
RE/Moral education		Shyness, cleverness, reliability, etc.; self-assessment	Duty/responsibility to parents	Religion; friendship groupings; duty/responsibility	Likes and dislikes; duty/responsibility

Suggested techniques: creative writing, poetry; drama; taping of mock interviews; photography and film-making.

the whole project. This has avoided the possibility of children who have been absorbed in several activities in some depth from missing out on what other groups have achieved. It also enables the teacher to use the exhibition as a focus for the important discussion work which will follow.

Obviously, the more techniques that are used for exhibition purposes, the more demanding and challenging the exhibition becomes to both exhibitors and spectators. Films, tape-recordings, photographs, models, etc., can be stimulating additions to the more conventional diagrams, graphs, creative writing, drawings and paintings, etc.

The school profile

AIMS

1   To inculcate awareness of others in relation to themselves, and vice versa.
2   To enable children to learn the 'tools of the trade' for later surveys of area.
3   To improve basic skills of observation and communication (e.g. looking and listening, writing, speaking).
4   To improve understanding of school as a community.

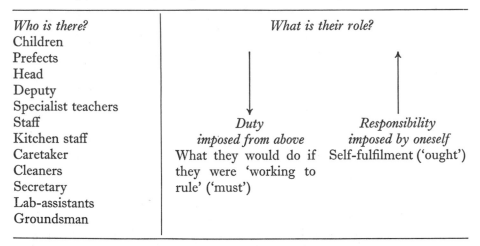

Who is there?	*What is their role?*	
Children		
Prefects		
Head	↓	↑
Deputy		
Specialist teachers		
Staff	*Duty*	*Responsibility*
Kitchen staff	*imposed from above*	*imposed by oneself*
Caretaker	What they would do if	Self-fulfilment ('ought')
Cleaners	they were 'working to	
Secretary	rule' ('must')	
Lab-assistants		
Groundsman		

It would be necessary to consider the school from every conceivable point of view: physical structure, numbers of pupils and staff, distribution of staff, sizes of various age-groups, number of clubs and societies and size of their membership, number who take school meals, the roles of all the people who live and work in the school, and perhaps most importantly, their relationship to each other.

Clearly, there is scope for work on many aspects of the school curriculum and

134

SUGGESTED SCHOOL PROFILE

Plan	Surveys	Interviews	Relationships (socio-dramas)
1 Diagrammatic plans of school		Interview techniques, mock interviews, tapes of interviews	head/pupil
2 Staff distribution according to subjects	Subject rooms and register rooms	Interviews with heads of departments	
3		Question sheets for interviews	
4		Interviews with all people named on separate sheet	how we deal with offenders
5 Wall chart of profile-group		Photographs of interviewees	
6 Structure of classes (i.e. streaming and numbers)	Numbers of boys/girls		
7 Model of school	Nationalities	Interviews with representatives of different cultural groups for cultural differences, etc.	pupil/pupil
8	Attendance and punctuality		prefect/junior
9	How children travel		
10	Careers		
11 Ancillary staff distribution	School meals, litter, tuck shop	Recording answers and tabulation	school meals supervisor/pupil; caretaker/pupil
12	School societies, sports	Open forum of representatives of all people interviewed	

a need for co-operation between various departments, so that, conceivably, a real team-teaching project could arise. Preferably, a teacher who takes the group concerned for a number of lessons would act as co-ordinator.

The school profile sheet reproduced is not a blueprint, but merely an attempt to structure the project. Numbers 1–12 refer to the chronological sequence of the various tasks, although naturally there would be a need for flexibility because of some of the more obvious overlaps. Of course, schools would no doubt feel that many other aspects of school life could be considered. I feel that an exhibition at the end of the project could give the children a feeling of achievement, a further goal to aim for, and a more coherent picture of the whole project.

The area profile

A profile of an area may comprise some of the following:

(a) *Where we live*
Describing our neighbourhood: residential, factories, shops, etc.
The street: neighbours, ages, children.
Our customs: the way we live, weekends and holidays.
The way we come to school: bus, cycle, walking, car.
Neighbours in difficulty: the elderly, cripples, chronic sick.
Local characters.
Relations who live near: grandpa, grandma, uncles, aunts.
Friends.

(b) *How we play – what do we do after four o'clock*
Clubs we belong to: what we do there, games, how many attend, age-range, how often we go, whether we enjoy it, how we would improve it.
Places to play unsupervised: parks, waste ground, football pitches.
Where we meet our friends; the gang, what we do.
Where we are not allowed to play and why; where we or others are likely to get into trouble, danger areas, old buildings, railway lines, private property.
Where do we go on Saturday afternoons? What for? Alone, or with friends?
Are we likely to get into trouble? Why?

(c) *Local problems*
Dangerous roads, derelict areas.
Transport: bus shelters, frequency of buses, bus stops.
Old people: housing problems, bad landlords.

136

(d) *Authority and you*
Where is the police station in our area?
Relationships with the police. Policeman's usual beat. Does he move us on, and why?
Local 'busybodies', park-keepers, uniformed attendants.
Relationships with people near where we play: old people, do they tell us to play elsewhere, and why?
Any unpleasant people who frighten or chase us.

(e) *The church*
What church do we go to: how many go, which denomination, do we go alone or with friends?
What local charities are there? Do we help? How?

(f) *Emergency services*
Ambulance station, hospital, fire station.
Local people who help in emergencies.
Civil Defence, Red Cross, St John Ambulance.

(g) *The leaders in our area*
Who are they? The spokesmen for other people's problems: the councillor, the vicar, the youth leader, the doctor, any others.

(h) *Where we meet*
Where do the grown-ups, our parents, meet to gossip: the street corner, local shop, the pub, the church hall, any other places?
Where do the old people go to meet? Where do the young wives with babies go?

(i) *Newcomers and minority groups*
Are there any newcomers in our neighbourhood: Indians, West Indians, Italians, Irish? How have they been made welcome? Do people talk about them, are they disliked, do we play with their children, why not?
  Are there any gipsies: where do they live, are they made welcome, if not who moves them on? What do we think of them, have we met any? Are there any tramps or people sleeping rough? Where? How do they live, where do they get their money? Are they made welcome by our neighbourhood, have we spoken to them, are they disliked, why?

Appendix B Syllabuses and reports from participating teachers

1. THE FOURTH-YEAR SYLLABUSES FOR SCHOOLS A, B, C AND D

School A – The thinking behind our approach to social education

This outline syllabus is tentative, since it provides no more than signposts on the way. Since we do not know exactly where we are going, too much notice ought not to be taken of the signposts. We cannot know where we are going because our aim is social involvement, and active social involvement is the result of joint decision-taking. In the spirit of the *Dialogue* article,* we do not propose to try to impose our values (or anybody's values) on the pupils. We hope that they will gather information – some of it from us – and form their own values. What seems to us a cause for concern is not necessarily a cause for concern for them. However, there is evidence that their lack of interest in the Meadows Redevelopment scheme was due simply to ignorance of what it entails for them.

The timing is fortuitous. We could not have arranged that the redevelopment should come into general discussion precisely at this time, nor could we forecast that in 1970 *The Guardian* would run a series of articles on 'Survival in the Cities', nor that conservation, the quality of the environment and so on, would comparatively suddenly become matters of general interest. We did not engineer student unrest, the situation in Northern Ireland, etc. It would be foolish, though, not to make use of this series of events, since it is all part of 'what we are on about'.

How far is it possible to live in cities? Should we talk about 'Survival *of* the Cities'? It is impossible to believe that all is well; at the moment of writing some of our cities are choked, not only with motor vehicles, but also with rubbish uncollected for weeks. We cannot, or will not, pay adequately those who service our cities.

Many of us are opting out of city life by moving into suburbs or dormitory villages, thus repeating what has already happened in the USA. The decaying centres are left to the poor, including many immigrants. Those who earn their living in the city often do not pay the rates which keep it going. We are building a bomb which will explode in the not too distant future. Where large-scale redevelopment takes place, the new property is frequently beyond the means of the 'old' residents who are moved out to estates on the outskirts, often with heavily increased costs of transport. Those who cannot afford this solution have to be found older houses in yet other decaying or decayed areas. Is it inevitable that the process continues?

* 'Children and their community' by John Rennie, *Dialogue*, Schools Council Newsletter No. 6, autumn 1970.

138

It would be expecting a great deal of the pupils if we thought that they could determine the answers to problems to which, so far, no country appears to have found a solution. We hope that they will become aware and will not be apathetic. We want them to question their fate, to call planners to account. (It would be interesting to know how many designers of high-rise flats would not be seen dead in one.)

Social education is about people. We are hopeful enough to believe that it is not quite yet too late, although it must be nearly so, to make the cities fit to live in. In the last analysis, however, we are concerned about how people live with people. The environment is important, and the most important part of it is other people. For this reason, we wish to look at personal relationships (not used here as a synonym for sex education). How do groups of people function? We also wish to look at the world of work. Personal relationships at work are nearly as important, for most people, as those at home. We do not need any justification for these aims, but anyone who thinks we might better spend the time doing something else is invited to look at the figures for psychiatric illness, for crime, for divorce, for suicide, for family breakdown. These are all symptoms of social and personal relationships reaching the point of breakdown.

More readily accessible symptoms of alienation can be found almost daily in the correspondence columns of our newspapers. The following letter appeared in a local paper during the course of the project and was one of a series expressing similar sentiments:

'Not guilty – Three cheers for correspondent Indifferent. I do not care what happens in Africa, and I am sick of people trying to make me feel guilty about children, convicts, black people and slums. I earn what I get, and thanks to this government it will soon be more. Keep it up Ted. Another Indifferent, Arnold.' (Letter in *Nottingham Evening Post and News*, 5 November 1970.)

School B – Broadening the course in the fourth year

This course has been designed for lower stream fourth-year girls. It is the first year that this subject has been on the timetable for fourth-year pupils and therefore the ideas are only experimental.

The class concerned is the fourth stream of a five-streamed fourth-year (X, A, B, C, D). In their second and third years the girls had a social studies lesson every week. The second year was devoted to class and school profiles. In the third year the girls studied the area (i.e. Clifton Estate). The fourth-year scheme is a continuation and widening of these courses. This year the class has one afternoon per week (2 hours) allocated to social studies.

139

1. *Local work in Nottingham*
This is principally a local geography study of the development of Nottingham. It is dealt with very simply because of the ability of the girls. The work incorporates a visit to the older parts of the city, i.e. St Mary's Hill, Castle Rock, etc.

2. *Districts around Nottingham*
This section deals with the spread of the City of Nottingham into surrounding villages. In detail the development of Clifton Estate at the side of the original village. The beginnings of the Meadows, St Ann's, the village of Lenton, etc.

3. *New developments in the city*
This is designed to make the children aware of the present development in the city. Studied in detail:

> The Victoria Centre;
> St Ann's Redevelopment;
> Meadows Strategy Plan.

4. *Social effects of housing*
Study the design of houses and conditions in differing areas.

The effect of old housing, old school buildings, etc., especially on children. Contrast this with a visit to privately owned property – visit show houses on new building sites.

Much of this work can be dramatized. Other ideas:

> what makes a good home?;
> problem of moving house;
> settling into a new area;
> living in a block of flats;
> living in slum conditions;
> overcrowding – living in one room, etc.

5. *Different types of homes*
The idea of this section is to make the children realize the problems faced by people who do not live in a so-called 'normal family environment':

> children in homes – arrange a visit from children's officer;
> the homeless – study the work of Shelter;
> approved schools, Borstals, etc.

140

6. *Social problems*

In this section the social problems of drug addiction, mental illness and physical disability are dealt with. Use of films and discussions.

7. *Social relationships*

This section deals with attitudes to and prejudices about:

child/family relationships;
child/neighbour relationships;
boy/girl relationships;
marriage.

8. *The work crisis*

This section should help to overcome the 'gate' crisis. Visits to local factories, works, etc. (Boots, Players, hospital, knitwear factories). To help overcome 'the fear of the first job' – invite old girls to come back to school to answer the questions about starting work (involving as many different types of job as possible).

School C – A course for Newsom pupils

INTRODUCTION

For some four-and-a-half years, the fourth-year leavers have, on Monday, Tuesday and Thursday afternoons, been grouped within the Newsom department for studies based on half-termly themes such as 'World of Work', 'Law and Order', 'Needs', etc. The success of the department's work, especially in its earlier years, was that the youngsters benefited from knowing that someone cared sufficiently to plan their final year at school, and to help them over the difficult transition from school to work. Within the last eighteen months, however, it has become increasingly evident that the Newsom department can no longer work in isolation, or for that matter work successfully without proper preparation in the third year. Also the content of many of the themes needs to be radically revised.

This next year, September 1970, will see unstreaming, started some three years ago, reach the fourth year. Many of the social problems so evident in the past no longer exist and the leavers are an altogether more integrated and socially balanced group. Although banding into Newsom and CSE still occurs, the CSE humanities (English and social studies) is now blocked on the same three afternoons, so affording the fourth-year teachers the opportunity for a more integrated approach to CSE and Newsom. The emphasis is to be more on types of courses rather than just on leavers and CSE courses.

141

It is undoubtedly necessary for those leaving at Easter and in the summer of 1971 to have the opportunity for a detailed study of the 'World of Work' in the autumn and spring terms, while those staying on for a fifth year can make a similar study much later. Also, especially without Mode III CSE, there will be occasions when a more academic approach is needed with the CSE groups. However, the opportunity exists for a closer co-operation between CSE and Newsom, and with the raising of the school-leaving age in 1972/73 this co-operation will be an asset towards the building up of Mode III integrated studies, and the introduction of courses, particularly in the fifth year. There will, however, always be a need for the less able among the fourth and fifth years to follow courses specially designed to suit their needs and abilities. These Newsom courses must provide the stimuli to provoke individual and group studies, but more important, the stimuli to provoke group discussion and a social awareness of the problems they will meet, and may already have met. This social awareness should never be thrust upon individuals or groups, but cultivated during discussions, visits, etc.

AIMS

The following outline of aims and schemes will change year by year, and is a guide only to the Newsom themes being studied during 1970/71.

1. To create a social awareness of the problems facing our society through a study of the themes 'world of work', 'man/woman relationships', 'prejudice', 'outsiders and scapegoats', etc.
2. To create outward-looking courses, the content of which can be adapted to suit individual needs and interests.
3. To allow the young people the opportunity for group studies and discussion linked to the themes.
4. To give some help with the difficult transition from school to work by giving experiences directly related to the problems of automation, retraining and increased leisure time.
5. To give the youngsters social experiences through visits (including 'careers' visits) and by arranging for speakers to come into school.
6. To bring about an improvement in the ability of these youngsters to tolerate other opinions, to be willing to examine and accept change where and when it is necessary, and above all to bring about an increased awareness of their role in society.
7. To improve their basic academic standards, with particular reference to their ability to read and interpret facts, to listen to and discuss other opinions and to write creatively.

142

8. Finally, remembering that:

> the value of educational experience should be assessed in terms of its total impact on the pupil's skills, qualities and personal development, not by basic attainments alone (Newsom Report)

the courses followed, and themes studied, should be purposeful in the eyes of the young adult, and be relevant and suitable to his needs.

The following outlines of themes are meant only as a guide, and it is expected that they will be adapted to suit individual groups. It is also expected that the content will be changed as we improve on our resources and techniques. Some of the outlines are in detail and this is a deliberate attempt to lay down a pattern of approaches.

Arrangements are now in hand for a series of conferences and parent evenings, and it is hoped these events will help to finalize plans for the course.

WORLD OF WORK

This is an outline of the theme; the exact timing of visits, etc., will be given to the staff involved at the beginning of September. For the first visits to places of employment, these have been divided into three sections:

1. September–October: group visits to be undertaken by every member of a particular group. These visits should be used to introduce each young person to the techniques of recording information and as a stimuli for group discussion. These visits, as with all of the visits, should be looked on as a social experience as well as being of career value.
2. November–February: smaller and more specialized visits when each member of the group will have the opportunity of opting for four or five out of some twenty visits.
3. February–April: unsupervised (by staff) visits individually or in small groups, to their chosen place of employment, or similar firm/shop.

The actual careers content in the course will depend on the value of the visits, the preparation and follow-up work, and allied subjects should be treated as much for their social as for their careers value. All this work should form part of a valuable experience, and discussion, drama, creative writing, etc., should hold equal parity with recording facts. Copies of the book *Work* by R. Dingwall will be made available to all members of the team and this has some excellent suggestions and background information for drama and discussion. Trade unions, wages, budgets, safety at work, types of jobs available, factory/store organization,

143

automation, retraining, first day at work, leisure, living away from home, interviews, letter writing, finding a job, etc., are all topics which can be dealt with effectively through drama, films, TV or literature extracts. Some form of stimulus will be made available for all these topics, and the dates mentioned in the following outline of work are only an approximate guide.

All the following books contain extracts, information and ideas based on this theme:

R. Dingwall, *Work* (Religious Education Press, 1970)

E. Jones, *Work and Leisure* (Pergamon, 1968)

H. Cunningham, *The Work We Live By* (Pergamon, 1968)

V. F. M. Garlick, *Out to Work: an Apprentice Looks at His Job* (Longman, 1966)

T. D. Black, *Work and Wages* (McGraw-Hill, 1969).

There is a linked assignment with this last book, and this should be used during the Easter term when it can serve as a preparation for leaving, and as a continuous piece of work for those involved in visits.

Outline of work

September: discussions about the types of work available in the area, wages (linked assignment sheet available), what work will be like (stimulus-extracts from *Work and Leisure*), personal assessment forms in readiness for interviews.

October: visits by careers officer, detailed preparation and follow-up for visits to: Boots, B.S.C., Lawrences, Meridian, Spray and Burgess, Players, etc.

November–January: more specialized visits to Bournes, Marshall Conveyors, N.C.B., *Evening Post*, Boots, B.S.C., Lawrences, Trent Concrete, Furse, Foremans, Ashworth Kirk, Metro Gas Meters, Dobsons, Bairnswear, Ericssons, bakery, etc. Work: searching for jobs, interviews (drama), letter writing, etc. Trade unions (end of October).

February–March: unsupervised visits to future places of employment. Work: safety at work, automation, etc. *Work and Wages* assignment.

Television programmes: BBC *Going to Work* – Mondays, 2.30–2.50. ITV *Working Together* – Thursdays, 2.30–2.50.

These programmes will be used (as for 1969–70) by the various groups as they suit individual needs. Where programmes have an obvious social implication as, for example, the BBC's dramatized plays about work, the staff will be informed in advance so that preparations through group discussions may be initiated. Thirty copies of the BBC's *Going to Work* pupils' pamphlets, for all

144

three terms, will be available. This last year, the BBC *Scene* programmes (Thursday, 2.05–2.30 p.m.) have been outstandingly well produced and an undoubted stimulus to discussion. It is impossible to build a detailed programme of work around this series because the very nature of the programme is to deal with topical events, as well as controversial themes on law and order, old age and war.

In future, the last two periods on a Thursday will be available to watch suitable programmes in this series. As much warning as possible will be given to the staff about the content of each programme; staff will be expected to prepare possible material in advance. Each group should be encouraged to produce a piece of folder work based on the various themes being studied in the programme, and this work can always be completed in Newsom English time. The aim behind these studies should be to supplement current work, and to broaden the pupils' horizons as much as possible. As an extra bonus such studies can provide interesting work for those who have completed careers or other studies, and allow them the freedom of following up other themes or topics.

In previous years, the autumn term has begun with a detailed study of law and order. Experience has taught us that this study leads to too many conflict situations before we have time to assess the individual members of our particular group. This year, for the first time, the pattern of the term has been changed so that we have time first to assess and mould our group and, second, to introduce them to the demands of group discussion.

LIVING IN GROUPS/OUTSIDERS AND SCAPEGOATS

A short study (4–5 weeks) through discussion, film clips and literature of the various group loyalties each person faces.

A more detailed study of the outsiders and scapegoats of our society. Discussions of the need for scapegoats, including reference to Jews, immigrants, etc., and studies of teenage problems. The visits to the Mapperley Hospital and the follow-up film and talk will be used within this theme.

Further details, including lists of films, speakers and literature will be made available before the end of term.

The two studies described above will afford the groups plenty of opportunity for creative writing and socio-drama but, more important, they will introduce the youngsters to the group discussion situation.

The very nature of this work will 'poach' on themes to be studied later in the year, e.g. prejudice, teenage problems, drugs, etc., and the group teachers should encourage the youngsters to take a broad rather than a narrow topic-based view of the study. It is also worth mentioning that this type of work, involving stimuli (films or literature) and discussion may best be tackled in short bursts rather than a whole afternoon. Staff may arrange this to suit their needs and interests, and it may well be that some of the careers work (personal assessment, types of job, etc.) can be introduced during these afternoons. It would also seem appropriate that the reading of William Golding's *Lord of the Flies* should be started towards the end of September or the beginning of October as an introduction to the study of 'Law and Order', but the exact timing and choice of novels (John Christopher's *The World in Winter* and *Death of Grass* could be used) will be left for individual teachers to decide.

LAW AND ORDER

Aims:

To encourage creative work by the use of films, speakers, literature and discussion; to bring about an awareness of the problems of hooliganism, capital punishment, law reform, arming the police, crowd behaviour and other controversial issues, through a detailed study of law and order; to create situations where the youngsters are encouraged to question and discuss the various aspects of law and order.

Materials available:

No. of copies

30	Stan Barstow, *The Desperadoes* and other short stories (Michael Joseph, 1961)
60	William Golding *The Lord of the Flies* (Faber, 1954)
20	John Christopher, *Death of Grass* and *The World in Winter* (Penguin, 1970 and 1965)
30	A. Higgs, *Law and Order* (Longman, 1967)
40	K. Calthrop, *Crime and Punishment* (Pergamon, 1968)
60	Connexions: *The Lawbreakers* (Penguin, 1969)
20	*Going to Work* 'The Police' (BBC pamphlet)
30	*Protest* (SCM pamphlet)
30	*Courts* (Law Society pamphlet)
40	Crime and Punishment ⎱ information sheets devised
30	Capital Punishment ⎰ by project staff and teachers
40	JP Training
2	Kit, including a record of a court proceeding.
30	Alan Sillitoe, *A Sillitoe Selection* (Longman, 1968)
20	Stan Barstow, *The Human Element* (Longman, 1970)

146

Visits: City and county magistrates' courts; county quarter session.

Visitors: Mr S—— from Beechwood Remand Home; police forum; Borstal officer from Lowdham Grange; security officer; probation officer; magistrate (JP); police frogman and dog-handler; prison officer.

Films: BFI film study extracts – *Lord of the Flies, Z Cars*, etc.; Sound Services – *The Stable Door* and *Bash and Grab*; *Police Dog*; BBC – *Last Bus*.

A suggested outline

Brief study of the history of the police, and history of crime and punishment; need for a police force; what exactly is law and order?

Police forum – group involvement; background – the modern police force.

Police frogman and dog-handler; the specialized aspects of police work, e.g. drugs.

Film extracts (BFI) and reading of extracts from *Lord of the Flies* – 2–3 weeks; breakdown of law and order.

Magistrates' court – after 2–3 weeks: (1) preparation, court system, with particular reference to magistrates' court and procedure; (2) follow-up, discussion of cases, detailed work on cases, verdicts, personal opinions, etc; (3) record of court hearing, newspaper accounts.

Drama, based on *The Desperadoes*, and using magistrates' court visit. See A. Higgs, *Law and Order*, for ideas.

Films: *The Stable Door* and *Bash and Grab* to stimulate discussion about crime and punishment. Drama: extracts from *Crime and Punishment* anthology.

Talk by JP (can be arranged to coincide with court visit), discussion about training, case histories using information sheet prepared by project.

Other speakers can be used to suit individual needs.

The group should be encouraged to keep a diary of events and produce creative work when it is appropriate. Discussion and drama should form the core of this work, but factual work should also be tackled where it is appropriate.

The actual details of the study are left to the individual group teachers. It may well be found, for instance, that a further visit to a magistrates' court, with a detailed piece of drama based on this visit, and the reading of *The Desperadoes*, takes up a lot of time, but if this is what the group is interested in and involved with, then the remainder of the suggested lines of inquiry can be adapted. Full use should be made of the extracts and books available, and staff are advised to read them if they are unfamiliar with their content. To stimulate group discussion, the Penguin Connexions topic book, *The Lawbreakers*, will be useful.

School D – 'Living in groups'

The situation in School D was a little different from the other schools in that John Rennie and Wyn Williams did the teaching themselves. The syllabus designed has been particularly concerned with the question of relationships between class members themselves and between the youngsters and the project staff. It is recognized that the emphasis is likely to be different in the case of teachers who know their classes very well. Here is their report.

First term
The emphasis has been upon 'Living in Groups' – particularly their own peer groups.
   Major objectives have been:

(a)   The establishment of a class committee which would take over responsibility for things like collecting homework, running sessions when we are not present, noting and putting forward suggestions for action made by the class.
(b)   The recognition by the class that we valued them behaving at all three social ages – child, adolescent, and adult – and that we were willing to change our behaviour as they changed theirs. In particular, when they wanted to behave as adults and conduct their own affairs, we would withdraw.
(c)   To get them to recognize the three types of group and when they ought to operate and how youngsters could act to change or influence events.

These objectives we saw as more important than any attempt to teach any particular subject-matter. The subject-matter we used was, therefore, designed to *illustrate* and *stimulate* them to think about the objectives stated above. We used:

1.   A film, *Last Bus,* to develop the ideas about types of group and the possibilities of altering the ending by action on the part of conductor and passengers.
2.   A poem, 'Street Gang' by Harry Webster, to illustrate the group values.
3.   Slides of a Fulani (African tribe) initiation ceremony to show the importance attached to belonging to a group and what is involved.
4.   Socio-drama to illustrate how an outsider can become a scapegoat.
5.   Another film to stimulate interest in people who are outsiders in our society – *I Think They Call Him John.*
6.   Man/woman relationships as an end to the term because conflict between
148

the boys and girls is apparent within the class. Here we discuss women's rights and five spheres of relationship between men and women.

Second term
The emphasis was on developing the interest in groups in society who are outsiders in one sense or another, and what has been and what can be done to assist them.

The outline syllabus we used for this term is reproduced below.

Conclusion
The intended emphasis was on how the group could turn outwards to look at the world outside the school. In reality it has been necessary to spend a term in getting the class to be aware of themselves and building their confidence in controlling themselves and taking action within the confines of the class. It may be possible to turn our attention outwards next term.

Week 1   Attack on the class group leading to discussion of different types of group. Election of class committee as the class disciplinary body; socio-drama.
Homework:

(a) What groups do you belong to?
(b) Which is most important to you?
(c) Did you choose the group or did they choose you?
(d) Who are the leaders in the group?

Week 2   Follow-up to homework.
Socio-drama of class committee.
Written work: log of work attempted this term.

Week 3   Why we live in groups (protection, solidarity, companionship, identity, etc.); examples.
Behaviour of groups – the mob, vandalism, teenage sub-cultures.
Film: *Last Bus* – BBC.

Week 4   The group's values.
Poem: 'Street Gang' by Harry Webster.
Where do the values come from?
Leadership: *Going to Work* 'Apprenticeship' – BBC.

Week 5   Those outside the group – scapegoats; socio-drama.
Written work: poems.

Week 6   Discussion on three questions:

(a) What behaviour is expected from you by teacher in school?
(b) What is your behaviour towards each other when teacher is not present?
(c) What happens when you fail to obey rules?

149

Week 7   Socio-drama – the newcomer.
Week 8   Written work on scapegoatism.
Week 9   Film: *I Think They Call Him John.*
Weeks 10, 11 and 12   Man–woman relationships.

Each week, time to be given for the children to write up their log of the work they are doing. Creative writing as indicated. Wall newspaper to be built up of articles, photographs, headlines from press, magazines, etc., of appropriate nature.

2. REPORTS FROM PARTICIPATING TEACHERS

a   Introducing social education as part of a broad humanities programme

As a first thought the introduction of any 'new' subject into the school timetable seems to me a detrimental step, especially at a time when we are trying to cut down the subject barriers and thus (we hope) create a more meaningful approach to educating the young adult. In any case, as the situation exists in most schools, another subject fighting for two periods on the timetable is surely going to be a non-starter. It seems to me that social education has far more chance of acceptance if it can be introduced to reinforce an already accepted course or subject, e.g. English, social studies or a humanities course. Also, and this becomes more of a problem with raising the school-leaving age, integrated social education stands a much better chance of being accepted as part of an examination programme, than it would if it were a separate subject. A Mode III CSE social studies course could, for instance, include most of what we think of as social education, providing it was examined as part of a programme of continuous assessment.

Further, to teach social education as a separate subject implies new subject-matter, whereas to my mind it is not so much the newness that makes social education so revolutionary as its approach to social problems. Integrated into the humanities programme this new approach has far more chance of being implemented, and also allows time for follow-up, and more scope for completing detailed surveys, individual studies, discussion, etc.

One of the main advantages of having social education integrated into a humanities programme is that the youngsters are allowed more time for linked creative work. Many of our youngsters can never fully understand the problems of being old or alcoholic, for instance, because they seem far too remote, but given the right sort of stimuli – such as *I Think They Call Him John* (Contemporary Films) or the Australian film *A Man with a Problem* – and follow-up discus-

150

sion, it is surprising how vividly many of the youngsters can write about being old, etc. Also – and this was as a direct result of youngsters being given the scope of an integrated approach – a new line of attack, which in this case was conservation and pollution, can start directly from pupil involvement in other aspects of social education, i.e. the area profile. Because I had the time within the humanities programme (12 periods a week) to devote to detailed follow-up, a worth-while piece of work (lasting 11 weeks) was tackled immediately, with the whole weight of the form's English and environmental studies time thrown in to aid those youngsters who needed time for field work. I can hardly imagine a similar study coming out of a two-period social education subject.

As a final point, social education can always be introduced into a humanities programme as another 'topic', and its arrival in the school curriculum can thus escape the notice of the 'anti-social-education brigade'!

Of course, introducing a new element or approach into an already established programme has its problems. It is more than likely that you will hear the anguished cries of 'Oh, I've been doing this for years' because they may well have been doing a social 'thing' without there having necessarily been any education. Also trying to gain acceptance for a new approach in an already planned and successful humanities scheme can lead to big problems with the staff. Just because a school has a well-organized humanities scheme does not, of course, preclude staleness and even a certain reactionary attitude among the staff. This will always be a problem, and introducing social education into an already existing scheme did lead to certain difficulties over changes to the subject-matter, and even more over the approach. When staff are working together as a team, and this we take as synonymous with a humanities scheme, planning often takes place a term and even six months ahead. Therefore, any attempt at introducing social education, for instance, would have to take this into account. In this particular case not enough preliminary consultation led to difficulties with planning, and early rejection by some staff.

b Introducing social education into a subject-based timetable

Accepting that no education exists which is not social, and that social education goes on whenever people are together, and even when they are not – there is a form of social interchange in the reading of a book, for example – there are certain difficulties which may be met when an attempt is made to introduce something called social education into a school. These could be placed in two categories: (a) attitudes of mind, and (b) organizational and other difficulties 'caused' by the existing situation in the school. It could, of course, be argued that

151

the latter are 'caused' by social education, since they do not exist before it appears on the scene.

ATTITUDES OF MIND

In this particular situation, the noticeable attitudes are more likely to be hostile than not, at any rate in the case of the teachers. The attitude of the headteacher must be taken for granted as pro rather than con, since if he or she is against social education it is not likely to begin at all in the school. On the other hand, however much support is given by the head, there is no absolute guarantee that the newcomer will be welcome. The attitudes of teachers are not that easily altered. There will probably be a fairly large group of teachers who are, for one reason or another, neither particularly in favour nor particularly against. This group will usually give some assistance when they are asked, and when they can see the relevance (in terms of their subject or interests) of the work in hand. The enthusiasts need not be dealt with here, so we are left with the 'hostiles'.

These can also be divided conveniently into groups according to the main features of their display of hostility, but whatever the overt nature of their objections, there is a definable basic state of mind present in them all.

(i) Authoritarians may feel threatened by the freedom of expression (of the pupils) and by the pupil–teacher exchanges which are essential to our conception of social education.

(ii) Strongly subject-orientated teachers may be anxious about parts of the syllabus which can be 'missed' if time is given over to social education.

(iii) Those whose 'discipline' is only just maintained feel even less secure when they come into contact with pupils who are used to expressing themselves fairly freely. Pupils will deliberately exploit this situation.

(iv) There may be fear for the 'reputation of the school' (i.e. of the staff), and fear that pupils may 'let down the school' (i.e. the staff). There may also be anxiety in case pupils injure themselves while out of school (or in it) during unsupervised activities.

It will be clear, I hope, that the state of mind common to all these is one of anxiety and insecurity, although this is not the place to dwell upon its genesis. I will say only that however right Richard Hauser may be in his contention that we are moving into a shame-culture, my own feeling is that there is still an enormous amount of guilt. This is not, and is not intended to be, an indictment of any teachers or, for that matter, of their state of mind. This era has already been dubbed the 'Age of Neurosis' (e.g. by William Barrett), and teachers are a part of it.

152

Along with others, I have already referred several times to social education as a scapegoat and also as a polarizer. Where considerably different attitudes already exist (and they nearly always do) social education will undoubtedly polarize them very strongly, as will anything which threatens, or appears to threaten, the status quo. Other such issues would include team-teaching, IDE (interdisciplinary enquiry work), the abolition of corporal punishment, etc. Social education is particularly likely to be made a scapegoat because pupils will have more opportunity to make decisions, and will inevitably make more mistakes which will be cited as 'evidence' that they are worse than they were in the Golden Age before. Worse, pupils will be condemned in advance for things they might do given the chance. What is happening is that latent anxieties are being verbalized. No amount of explaining will remove these anxieties, since they are not really concerned with social education at all. It may be possible to allay some of the more overt fears.

The concept of social education assumes that attitudes *can* be changed. We ought not to overlook pupil attitudes. Some pupils, particularly those who like taking decisions and those who have abilities which are not much encouraged by the 'normal' set-up, will welcome it. Others, especially those who do not like taking decisions, may not. The pupils are not a major problem because their attitudes are less rigid. If this last assumption is invalid, we are in a hopeless situation, since the whole concept of education rests upon it. It is difficult to know what to do about teacher attitudes, but the only feasible answer seems to lie in a thorough explanation of what we hope to do *before* we begin to try to do it. The probable difficulties ought to be made clear. We also ought to succeed; there is nothing like success. For some considerable time it seems likely that in many schools social education will not be possible without the support of some body outside the school. The universities are uniquely placed for this function. In spite of the common accusations that universities are ivory towers and places where academics discuss questions as relevant to real living as the number of angels who could dance on the head of a pin, they still have a great deal of prestige. It is ironic that accusations about lack of relevance to real living should come from – of all places – schools. There remains the problem of translating the theories evolved in the universities, where people have time to think, into actual schemes of work for use in the schools, where people do not have time to think.

To turn to organizational and other difficulties: if social education is to be introduced into a subject-based timetable, it is really a matter for the head to say which subject(s) shall lose the time. I am not in favour of chopping social education into bits to be served up as 'geographical SE', 'historical SE' or – perish the thought – 'scientific SE'. To do this would certainly be to lose the

153

social education. As to which subject should lose the time, I am neutral, since I believe that no subject does anything as important as social education. In practice, then, a definite part of the week should be designated as social education on the timetable. If other teachers will give the time as necessary (some will), it can be spread over into other subjects. It is difficult to say how much time is required, since the requirement expands and contracts. In practice, I have found that even teachers strongly opposed to what they conceive social education to be will give time if the work seems useful, or if – as in the case of an interview outside school – it is obviously necessary to gain extra time.

Where integrated studies appears on the timetable, it is possible to obtain a flexible allocation of time for social education. It is also true that teachers who are prepared to do integrated studies are likely to view social education favourably. It ought to be made clear that social education is hard work.

Examination candidates pose a problem. They may regard social education as a welcome break from their usual work, or they may see it as a break of a different kind – a waste of their time which ought to be used for exam-passing. I hope that social education does not itself become an examination subject, at any rate as examinations are ordered at present. What bothers me here is not so much *what*, but *who*. Who is to decide that A is better socially educated than B? Immediately the question is posed in this form its absurdity is apparent. None of us is socially adept in all possible circumstances. Social 'competence', however defined, is a changing quality, because it is inherent in *relationship*. Few of us could socialize with an angry lion.

c   The class profile

Aim: to introduce 3D (an unstreamed form of thirty-five boys and girls) to the study of the school profile;
to introduce them to the techniques of collecting, interpreting and displaying information;
to give them a sense of identity with the form;
to allow freedom of movement within the various groups.

Method: Using the blocked time available for English/environmental studies, to study the form in detail and over a short period of time.

INTRODUCTORY LESSON

14 October
(a) The form, which is used to working on group assignments, projects and drama, and also works very well in a fairly fluid situation, was told that the

154

pupils were going to find out about themselves and the form before attempting the school profile.

(b) They all made up a questionnaire and their ideas were incorporated into a class questionnaire which they answered for homework.

PREPARATION

(a) The class were given the choice of the aspect of the profile they wished to find out about and they were allowed to work with friends. There were approximately twelve groups at the start, but the situation was extremely fluid and they constantly changed.

(b) Necessary equipment (stationery, card, etc.) was made available, and also a weighing machine. Thus a prompt start was made in the afternoon.

PROFILE

15 October, 3 × 40 minutes, Wednesday afternoon.

Facts
1. Height and weight of every member of the form.
2. Survey of likes and dislikes, under various categories (decided by the group).
3. Features – colour of eyes, length of hair, shape of mouth, etc.
4. Hair – samples, colours.
5. Shoes – size, type, colour and make.
6. Fingerprints and signatures.
7. Favourite TV programmes.
8. Religions.
9. Map to show where the class spent their holidays over the last three years.
10. Map to show where everyone lives.
11. Map to show place of birth of parents.
12. Survey of hobbies and interests.

28–29 October
Most of the work completed by Wednesday afternoon.
Written work on the group work:

account of work undertaken, recording of facts and results obtained;
are the facts collected useful and could they have been represented in a clearer or more efficient manner?;
what do you think of the work undertaken?

155

Observations

Most pupils enjoyed the further experience of working in groups at their chosen study, and produced work of a high standard. The work displayed was as good as the form usually produce, particularly when they are working on 'self-directed' assignments. Despite the occasional spelling error (on the maps, wall charts, etc.) the written work was thoughtful and the majority thought the profile was an enjoyable experience and interesting, though many could not see its usefulness. It was evident, however, that most children worked extremely well with each other and found out many interesting facts about fellow members of their form. It was their majority conclusion, and mine as well, that this study was only useful over a short period of time as an experience of working in groups. Some admitted that they had learnt useful techniques and methods of presentation, and particularly enjoyed the freedom of planning and presenting their own line of inquiry.

The 'exhibition' work produced, considering the short period of time allowed, was up to the form's usual standard and a few groups (for example, the one which made a 24-hour clock to represent time of birth, hair samples, facial features, etc.) revealed a refreshing originality and vitality.

My own opinion is that as a short study the form profile was a valuable experience which should obviously be attempted in the first year (summer term) or early second year. As an introduction to the school profile, and some of the techniques which would be involved in this study, it was a success. Finally, it once more proved to me the value of an unstreamed class working in groups on self-directed work within a chosen theme. The drama and discussion follow-up was average for the form. It did not appear to provide any different stimulus.

Appendix C   Evaluation: additional data

1. QUESTIONNAIRE ON ATTITUDE TO SCHOOL

Final form of questionnaire

Please answer all the questions by putting a tick in the column of your choice. If you do not understand a question or find difficulty with it, put a tick in the 'uncertain' column.

Thank you.

		Yes	No	Uncertain
1.	I shall be sorry to leave my class.	☐	☐	☐
2.	I have no friends I like very much in my class.	☐	☐	☐
3.	We enjoy ourselves in our class.	☐	☐	☐
4.	I have a best friend in my class.	☐	☐	☐
5.	There are very friendly children in my class.	☐	☐	☐
*6.	I would like to get away from the children in my class.	☐	☐	☐
*7.	Our teacher treats us as if we are babies.	☐	☐	☐
8.	The teacher helps the slow ones in a nice way.	☐	☐	☐
*9.	I get told off by my teacher.	☐	☐	☐
10.	I find it easy to talk to my teacher.	☐	☐	☐
11.	Teacher is interested in me.	☐	☐	☐
*12.	The teacher expects some boys and girls to do hard work while others do easy work.	☐	☐	☐
13.	I like school.	☐	☐	☐
*14.	Going to school is a waste of time.	☐	☐	☐
15.	We have interesting lessons in school.	☐	☐	☐
16.	I dislike children who are noisy in class.	☐	☐	☐
*17.	It is nice to fool about in class.	☐	☐	☐
18.	I like to get on with my work quietly.	☐	☐	☐
*19.	I do not like teachers who are strict.	☐	☐	☐
*20.	I think the prefects in our school are too bossy.	☐	☐	☐
21.	I think school uniform is a good idea.	☐	☐	☐
*22.	I like children to get me into mischief.	☐	☐	☐
*23.	I like children to tell jokes in class.	☐	☐	☐
24.	I am an easy sort of person for other children to get on with.	☐	☐	☐
25.	I think people like working with me.	☐	☐	☐
*26.	I never seem to get much right in school.	☐	☐	☐
27.	I think I am important in our class.	☐	☐	☐
*28.	Other children in our class think I do not count.	☐	☐	☐
29.	I think I am pretty good at school work.	☐	☐	☐
*30.	When I have a row with my friends it is usually my fault.	☐	☐	☐

* Negatively scored

Calculation of sub-scale scores

1. *Acceptance of school ethos*
   Total of scores for items 16, 17, 18, 21, 22, 23.
2. *Friendly relations with class*
   Total of scores for items 2, 3, 5 and 6 doubled, plus scores on items 1 and 4.
3. *Self-concept as successful pupil*
   Total of scores in items 26, 27, 29, doubled, plus total in items 11, 13 and 28.
4. *Appreciation of teacher*
   Total of scores in items 1, 8, 10, 11, 13, 15.
5. *Self-concept as socially acceptable*
   Total of scores in items 24, 25, 28, doubled, plus total in items 5, 27.
6. *Absence of self-concept*
   Total of scores in items 14, 26, 28, plus score for item 30, doubled.

Attitude to school: factor analysis (Varimax rotation)

Decimals omitted. Loadings shown only when significant at 0·05 level.

| | | | | *Factors* | | | | |
Item	I	II	III	IV	V	VI	VII	VIII
1		26			−40			
2		36			15			
3	−20	36			−12			
4		28				−23		
5		52			−12		14	
6		56	16					
7	15	14	47	12	−17			
8			13		−44			
9	23		31		−10*			
10					−54			
11	17			22	−48			
12		11	38					−12
13	32	29		13	−38			
14	20	24	13		−22		−11	13
15	11	29	10*		−36	−13		
16	35				−14			
17	59				−14			
18	51				−25			
19	11	−13				37		−11
20						43		
21	33				−24	(07)		−16

22	47							
23	49				14			11
24		19			−10*	−18	39	
25					−23		43	
26			20	45				13
27			−15	32	−13	13	12	
28		15	19	13			31	13
29				50				
30								32

* Rounded up from 098.

2. Further Examples of Interviews with Parents

Interview 1 (School A)

Mother interviewed. A widow with two children. The elder, a daughter, was training as a nursery nurse and was due to go to the Matlock Training College in September.

Her son had just obtained an apprenticeship at Oscroft's.

The house was a three-storey Victorian building in a redevelopment area. It was one of the few houses to be retained under the redevelopment order. The house was well-furnished and pleasantly decorated. It was clean and tidy and obviously well looked after. The mother was the owner/occupier. An expensive Hammond organ and a radiogram were the central features of the room in which the interview was conducted. The house had previously been without a bathroom but one bedroom was in the process of conversion. The mother appeared genuinely concerned about the confusion of the builders' materials and mess. Despite having only just returned from work, she made the interviewers extremely welcome.

Unlike the majority of interviews we conducted in which we had to press a series of questions, Mrs L—— responded to our initial question, regarding her son's attitude to school by taking over the interview and providing us with the information we sought with a minimum of prompting on our part.

She felt strongly that there had been a marked change in her son's attitude to school. This had become apparent from the beginning of his last year. Prior to this he had actively disliked school, played truant and had received adverse reports regarding his work and behaviour. He was now enthusiastic about school work, which he discussed in some detail with her and his recent reports showed a great improvement in his attitude, behaviour and academic achievement. This she considered attributable directly to the influence of his form master, Mr W——,

159

and the work Mr W—— had been doing with the Social Education Project. Her son had displayed great interest and involvement in this work. This was demonstrated by his desire to discuss his activities with great enthusiasm with his mother. (The project confirmed this statement.)

She attached great significance to the fact that the boy, although warned by his form master, careers master and the youth employment officer that with his lack of qualifications he stood little chance of securing an apprenticeship, was sufficiently mature to secure for himself interviews with three firms offering apprenticeships. He informed his mother that during the course of the interview he had been explicit about his attitude to school and his lack of application. He had also enthusiastically outlined his involvement in the Social Education Project. To their delight and surprise and the school's and YEO's amazement he was offered two of the three apprenticeships for which he had applied. He had accepted the offer from the firm of Oscroft's. The personnel officer of Oscroft's had contacted the mother to tell her how impressed he had been with her son – not merely with her son's involvement in the Social Education Project and his ability to discuss it, but also with his maturity in discussing his own shortcomings. The personnel officer expressed his admiration for the scheme and its obvious beneficial effect upon her son.

Mrs L—— was enthusiastic about the work being done, not merely for the change it had brought about in her own child but also for the social awareness it was capable of producing in the younger generation.

The interview lasted half an hour, during which time we played a minor role in face of her obvious enthusiasm for the project.

Interview 2 (School D)

The third eldest in a family of five. Both parents were interviewed, but the mother dominated the interview. The interview took place in the kitchen of a typical council house. The father was a miner.

They felt that their son's attitude to school had deteriorated during the last few months of his school career. The mother thought this was a natural consequence of being about to leave school. The boy had since left school and now worked for a multiple tailors.

The parents were interested in school activities but had no information about work in school or social education.

There was little evidence of an 'out-going' social involvement. The parents expressed the opinion when prompted that they were sympathetic to the idea of social education, but they appeared to feel that it had little relevance to them or their family.

160